RISKING THE TERROR

RISKING THE TERROR
RESURRECTION IN THIS LIFE

CHRISTINE M. SMITH

WIPF & STOCK · Eugene, Oregon

Wipf and Stock Publishers
199 W 8th Ave, Suite 3
Eugene, OR 97401

Risking the Terror
Resurrection in This Life
By Smith, Christine Marie
Copyright©2001 Pilgrim Press
ISBN 13: 978-1-60899-574-5
Publication date 10/5/2010
Previously published by Pilgrim Press, 2001

To Cathie Crooks, my beloved

Freedom

We raise our eyes in prayer
through the bars, darkly.

Together with a thousand prisoners in their cells
and with many more thousands in the larger
prison of our country.

We pray for freedom
and even more urgently, for life.

As nameless executioners salvage
those whom they used to merely torture and detain
and both children and parents
slowly but surely die
of sickness that has many names
and only one name.

We ask for faith
to see that death and prison are not forever
that life and freedom will prevail.

We ask for faith
to celebrate even while we mourn
knowing that death and prison
are already signs of a people's struggle
for freedom and life.

We raise our voices in prayer
through the bars, boldly
believing there will be an answer
as our people awaken.

Amen.
—Edicio de la Torre, 1984

Contents

Acknowledgments

I have been working on the ideas that are contained in this book for several years. I am the kind of writer who tests ideas many, many times before I believe they are worthy book material. Thus, my first expression of gratitude goes out to all those preachers across the United States and Canada who have listened to these ideas, enriched them, deepened them, and challenged me to develop them further. I owe profound thanks to preachers with whom I have shared time in Toronto, Kirkridge, San Anselmo, Halifax, Bedford, Minneapolis, Durham, Seattle, Bangor, Orlando, Duluth, and Atlanta. Your voices and your faithful ministries of word and sacrament have helped me not abandon this project. Thank you for your insights and encouragement.

There are three local places of ministry that have been highly influential in the shape and nature of this book: Casa de Esperanza, in St. Paul, an organization and shelter that advocates for Latina women and their children caught in violent relationships; Dwelling in the Woods, a hermitage in northern Minnesota that offers profound solitude and natural beauty; and Spirit of the Lakes United Church of Christ, my home church in Minneapolis, founded as a response to the religious and spiritual needs of lesbian, gay, bisexual, and transgendered people. In addition to these three local places of ministry, I give thanks for the love and respite in the presence and home of Leslie McGrath and Madir Pels in Truro, Cape Cod.

Toward the formation of this book, I am particularly grateful to the Atlantic School of Theology in Halifax, Nova Scotia. From April 22–24, 1998, I gave the Nicholson Lectures on preaching, and there I experienced wonderful hospitality and mutual learning. This event compelled me to organize the material I had and create much of what you will find in these pages. I am grateful to the school and to all the people who attended those lectures.

I am grateful to United Theological Seminary of the Twin Cities for a very generous sabbatical leave for the academic year 1997–1998. This gave me the time I needed to finally make a book out of the lectures, sermons, course notes, and new research that have occupied my passion and my thoughts for the past few years. I am proud to call United Seminary home, and I am enormously grateful to all the many people who support my writing and ministry in the world with their presence and their care. For the school's deep commitment to social justice, its affirmation of liberation theology, and its celebration of lesbian, gay, bisexual, and transgendered people's lives, I offer thanks. I am indebted to Jean Justice for her meticulous and skilled work with the manuscript for this book. While a student at United, she became the research assistant for this project. She is a professional editor in her own right, and the project has her distinct imprint on it from beginning to end.

I want to thank Rebecca Voelkel-Haugen for the constancy of her prayers and pastoral care and for being the kind of pastor in my life who empowers my Christian vocation in the world. I thank Martha Postlewaite for being a wonderful chaplain at the seminary and for her strong and tender pastoral presence at critical moments in my life.

My daily life in Minnesota is supported by a circle of very special friends. They rekindle my love for life, and they offer constant tenderness and support in times of struggle and growth. They help me laugh and play, they increase my faith, and they give my life roots and security. Thank you Elizabeth Bohun, Cathi Churchill, Kelly Connole, Denise DeVaan, Cathy Geist, Maggie George, Paula Lehman, Andrea Northwoods, Connie Nyman, Jane Sage, Carol Schoenecker, Joann Usher, and Kris Voelkel-Haugen.

I am deeply appreciative of the joy and love Marge and Bob Crooks have brought into my life. Though I cannot claim them as my legal parents-in-law, I treasure them as my beloved parents-in-law. I feel profound thanksgiving for my biological family, Betty and Raymond Smith, Pam, Charles, and Elizabeth, and for their love through all the years of my life.

Lastly, but most importantly, I raise my voice of gratitude to my life partner, Cathie Crooks. Everything changed the day she walked into my life. In a very real way, the last seven years of life with her have been a slow, steady, holy resurrection, and I am grateful beyond words. My life with Cath and our Weimaraner dogs, Gilly and Baylee, is joyous and full beyond what I could ever have imagined.

1

Resurrection in This Life

In a powerful theological and homiletical way, I think of this book as a kind of companion to my book, *Preaching as Weeping, Confession, and Resistance: Radical Responses to Radical Evil,* published in 1992. After working for many years on issues related to preaching and systemic injustice and oppression, I found myself urgently turning to the possibility of resurrection as that promise in the Christian faith that is strong enough to counteract and transform death itself. As a person of faith, I needed to believe in the enduring, uncompromising power of life again. As a practical theologian and preacher, I needed new language, new images, and new understandings that would enable me to be a more faithful proclaimer of God's resurrection life. This book is about that need and that quest.

In that quest, I have returned again and again to a particular quote by Anthony Padovano. I have prayed it, listened to it, been indicted by it, reflected upon it, and lived with it. I have hoped, and still hope, in some small measure, to follow it. It has served as a crucial guide and measure for my teaching, my writing, my preaching, my spirituality, and my life of faith. It seems the most fitting place to begin this book about the power and possibility of resurrection.

> Life, life is what you must affirm, no matter how painfully, even unwillingly. . . . You are reliable only when others ascertain they will always find life in your presence. Others must know you as faithful, faithful so often that when they wonder where life lives, they will think of you as one in whom life has made a home.[1]

This quote plunges me into perhaps the most important truth of the Christian faith for me: that *life* is what we are called to create, what we are called to struggle for, what we are called to dwell within, and what we are called to be. When I read it, I am reminded that in one's lifetime, it will take all of one's strength and passion to persistently affirm life. It would be an unspeakably holy accomplishment to be faithful enough that people might think of us "as one in whom life has made a home." Allowing life to make a home in us, affirming life—"no matter how painfully, even unwillingly," and being so reliable that others will always find life in our presence all have to do with resurrection life.

Let me say a few words about my own understanding of resurrection. I believe resurrection life to be of God. It is the indefeatable, eternal power of life that God has offered humanity, and infused into humanity, from the beginning of creation. It is also the power of life that resides within creation itself. It is the power of life that raised Jesus from the dead. It is the power of life that raised up the early Christian community. It is the power of life that raises up individuals and whole communities today. Resurrection is offered and given as sheer gift. Yet, at the same time, I believe there are human decisions we make, and actions we take, that can bring us closer to that power and nearer to the possibility of resurrection for all God's people and for creation itself. I believe that it is possible for human beings to embrace and receive this resurrection life and then to live it in ways that create and embody hope and life in the face of death and crucifixion.

The primary focus of my work is not upon the resurrection of Jesus, although this will be the focus of the fourth chapter. The focal point of this book is on the power and possibility of resurrection life in our world today, as well as some of the many ways individuals and whole communities experience and name it. To many of us who live privileged lives, some of the stories and images that appear in this book may seem far removed from our day-to-day lives. Yet I have tried to be faithful to what I believe is distinctive about resurrection: It is that which happens to us on the other side of various kinds of death. Could any of us deny that those who are oppressed, and those who suffer the violences of injustice, are the ones who most often experience the dramatic realities of death and of resurrection? I certainly believe that the power and possibility of God's resurrection is available to all, and that individual Christians, and whole communities together, need to learn how to name the deaths and the experiences of resurrection in our lives.

One of the most difficult challenges I needed to face in the writing of these pages is captured in a quote from Joanne Carlson Brown and Rebecca Parker's article, "For God So Loved the World."

Resurrection means that death is overcome in those precise instances when human beings choose life, refusing the threat of death. Jesus climbed out of the grave in the Garden of Gethsemane when he refused to abandon his commitment to the truth even though his enemies threatened him with death. On Good Friday, the Resurrected One was Crucified.[2]

If resurrection happens in the midst of gardens of Gethsemanes, deaths, and crucifixions, how will preachers avoid trivializing and romanticizing those very experiences of pain, suffering, and injustice? Might we conclude that if Jesus became the Resurrected One in the Garden of Gethsemane, maybe it was not so horrible that he was subsequently murdered? Or if the oppressed people of Guatemala experience resurrection right in the midst of all the death of racism and North American imperialism, then perhaps the genocide of that people is not so horrible? As preachers, how do we acknowledge that in the lived experience of many people death and resurrection are utterly intertwined, without diminishing for one second the horror of the death, the crucifixion, the suffering? Brown and Parker keep this challenge ever before us, and their words remind us that we must find new language for the relationship of Lent and Easter, new images for the relationship of death and resurrection, new ways of proclaiming the fullness and complexity of these interwoven realities. We will return to this challenge more explicitly in chapter five.

The passion I feel about resurrection has moved me to ask four questions, around which each of the next four chapters cluster:

1. What kind of spiritual and homiletical disciplines might move us as preachers closer to resurrection life? Here we explore what a resurrection spirituality looks like and what some of the practices of that spirituality might be for the preacher.

2. How might we resist the crucifixions that threaten to silence or defeat that resurrection life? In this chapter preachers are urged to take up the task of differentiating forms of human suffering and to enter into an ongoing struggle about God's presence and agency in the midst of crucifixions.

3. How can we recover a radical gospel that will sustain us in the quest for, and commitment to, resurrection life? In this chapter the preacher is urged to return to resurrection accounts in the gospel narratives and to discover them anew as stories of fear, struggle, and denial.

4. And, finally, how can we reimagine the nature and activity of resurrection life from the perspective of the oppressed and from the

perspective of those who have actually known death and resurrection? In this final chapter the preacher is immersed in the stories and moments of individuals and communities in hopes of expanding and deepening our fundamental understandings of resurrection.

At the conclusion of each chapter following, I have included a sermon that I believe embodies and reflects many of the homiletical issues raised in these pages. They are examples of my struggle to be faithful to various dimensions of resurrection life.

2

Refusing to Abandon Life

This chapter has everything to do with my own efforts to do what Anthony Padovano challenges: to be faithful enough to life that others might be able to find life in my presence. What I am about to share are the actual spiritual disciplines and practices I have discovered as I have sought to transform my own preaching into an act that faithfully resists injustice and serves the cause of liberation. These practices are some of the necessary disciplines that I have adopted as I keep trying to move my life and work into greater and greater solidarity with the marginalized and oppressed of this world.

In religious terms, these are some of the concrete spiritual and homiletical disciplines of a spirituality of resurrection that might undergird an entire preaching ministry. These spiritual disciplines promise to do what all spiritual disciplines do when they are faithfully practiced and integrated into the fabric of our lives. They will convert us. They will change our worldview. They will deepen our Christian faith. They will increase our compassion and mercy. They will immerse our lives in meaning. They will cause us struggle and pain. And they will bring about new life.

> One of the first spiritual and homiletical disciplines that is central to a resurrection spirituality is for the preacher to understand the primacy of social context and social location.

Social Context
Preaching is an act of ministry. It is done within particular social and religious contexts and is thoroughly influenced by the social location of the individual preacher. It is always contextual. It is a public act of theological naming.

What we have come to understand about language and naming is that those who *name* reality ultimately create, shape, and control the world in which we live. Because it is a powerful interpretive act, preaching constructs personal, social, and ecclesiastical reality.

White, western, male, Christian preachers, primarily in social contexts of privilege, often have taken the biblical text, the tradition, and the community of faith as the three primary starting places and points of focus for proclamation. For many preachers of social, economic, and cultural privilege, unquestioned authority is still given to scripture and tradition in the preaching act. Individual nurture, inspiration, and personal salvation are often the goals of such preaching. In this understanding of preaching, social analysis is not seen as primary and essential in a preaching ministry, and social and ecclesiastical changes are seldom the ultimate goal. Henry Mitchell, a prophetic African American preacher and writer, says it well: "There is a radical difference between listening to an essay designed to enlighten and listening to a Word desperately needed to sustain life."[1] In contexts of privilege, preaching may be more an act that enlightens, enriches, and inspires than it is an act that helps people actually survive.

This homiletical focus and context stands in real contrast to the particular witness of preachers who embrace liberation theology and who are preaching within contexts where people are struggling for justice and life. Liberation theologians and preachers seek to shape theology and the practice of ministry in response to the concrete realities of human suffering and oppression and toward a vision of liberation and restoration. If one preaches from within this liberationist perspective, whether one preaches in a context of privilege or a context of struggle and survival, the primary and ultimate agenda of liberation will inform homiletical content and method. This is certainly where I would locate my own theological and homiletical commitments.

Social Location

In North America many women and men today understand that almost every category of religion, faith, theology, and life has been defined and proclaimed as universal truth by white, privileged, Euro-American and Euro-Canadian males. With contemporary social and theological awareness, we know now that such generalizations perpetuate domination and injustice. In the craft of preaching there also have been too many generalizations, universal claims, and assumed truths spoken by the preachers who possess many levels of power and privilege. In light of our growing awareness about social location, contextuality, and the illusion of objectivity, we know that all conversations about preaching and the craft of preaching itself are significantly enriched and limited by the specificity of the speaker, author, or preacher.

We can no longer assume that any one methodology, style, or description can adequately name the vast array of differences among preachers. One's own critical awareness of social location will lead to a deeper understanding of the limitations and the particularities of one's social analysis, one's -theology, one's biblical hermeneutics, and one's ethical action in the world. Henry Mitchell has a particular social analysis of American culture from the perspective of ethnicity that I do not share. A person with a disability will read and interpret the healing narratives in the New Testament through a perspective I may never have. Poor Guatemalan Indians who are Christian may image God in ways I can barely imagine.

I am keenly aware that I speak as one voice: that of a white, Euro-American, economically privileged, highly educated, temporarily able-bodied lesbian who is a clergywoman within the United Church of Christ in the United States. My being white, Euro-American, economically privileged, highly educated, temporarily able-bodied, and ordained are all a part of what adds layers of privilege to my life. On the other hand, I am also aware that being a woman and being a lesbian add layers of discrimination and oppression to my life.

Being a woman means that I know the experience of being dominated, and that I continually feel afraid of male violence. Being a woman means that there are times when I feel invisible, devalued, objectified—even despised.

Being a lesbian means that I have spent most of my life afraid of hurting family, afraid of losing friends and colleagues, afraid of being attacked, afraid of being fired, afraid of losing my ordination. I have been denied jobs because I am a lesbian. I have been forced to leave the United Methodist Church because I could not be an open lesbian and keep my ordination. I know that no matter how many books I publish or how fine a scholar, teacher, or preacher I earnestly try to be, only a handful of seminaries in North America would even consider hiring an out lesbian faculty member like me. I left my primary calling, to be a parish pastor, because at the time I could not see a way it would be possible to be an out lesbian pastor in a local congregation throughout my lifetime.

Both the layers of privilege and the layers of oppression have shaped my life and have fundamentally influenced my life of faith, my theology, and my preaching. It is my responsibility to discern and to be truthful about the ways my own social location affects every aspect of my preaching. It is the responsibility of every preacher to be this truthful.

Vigilance about who one is and who one is not is a painfully difficult spiritual discipline. Furthermore, it is an absolute prerequisite for any genuine solidarity with others and for a preaching ministry of resistance and liberation. Vigilance about social location for me as a privileged North American preacher means that I must look at the ways my life, my actions, my theology, my worldview, and my preaching actively participate in the oppression of others. Vigilance about social location for me as a woman and as a lesbian means that each time I experience the direct impact of oppression and injustice, it sensitizes me, educates me, and raises my consciousness about all other kinds of oppression. This vigilance about social context and social location is an absolute foundational discipline for a resurrection spirituality.

Social Analysis

Because I believe that social context and social analysis are primary focus points for preaching, my homiletical work stands in very real contrast to that of many of my colleagues and to much of the contemporary literature in the field of homiletics. I respect current homiletical work on the nature of narrative and its relationship to homiletical method and design, but I do not concentrate my work on form and design. I am grateful for the work presently being done in relation to biblical literary forms and the way those forms come to expression in the content and shape of the sermon, but I do not focus my work primarily on the movement from text to sermon. I appreciate and draw upon dimensions of an inductive method in relation to the preaching event, a style that is less linear, less propositional, and less imperative, yet I wish to make more specific and explicit claims upon my own life and the lives of people in communities of faith than the inductive method suggests. I share a kinship with homiletical scholarship that focuses on the transformative power of language to reshape human consciousness and identity; however, I look to the fields of sociology and cultural anthropology to inform my social, homiletical, and theological analysis more than dimensions of linguistics. I find pedagogical commitments to develop a curriculum based on multicultural preaching to be absolutely crucial for the contemporary Christian church, but find myself moving beyond the celebration of cultural differences in a hope of uncovering and addressing the forms of systematic oppression that immerse some individuals and communities in privilege and others in violence and genocide. The boldest critique I bring to the contemporary field of homiletics is that much of the literature seems more concerned with form, style, textual analysis, and linguistics than with significant social analysis and the kinds of theological interpretation and concrete Christian actions and practices that flow from it.

Rather than beginning with scripture and tradition, liberationist preachers find the impetus of their preaching emerging from the larger social context of our individual and collective lives. These preachers attend first to the particular issues, social systems, pervasive cultural values, and ethics that structure the larger social and cultural world. Text, tradition, and faith community are important, but a hermeneutics of social context claims much of the agenda and commitments of a liberationist preacher.

Vigilance about the social context of the preaching event, the social location of one's self as preacher, and social analysis as primary agenda for an effective preaching ministry form the first cluster of spiritual and homiletical disciplines at the heart of a resurrection spirituality.

> A second spiritual and homiletical discipline of a resurrection spirituality is to critically examine the coherence and consistency of our theological commitments to see if they can lead us to a liberationist homiletic.

Preaching flows forth from a person's larger theological commitments. What one believes about the nature of ministry, the nature of God, the nature of the Christ, and the nature of the church will directly influence the substance and style of one's preaching ministry. If we are striving to be liberationist preachers, then we must look at our theological commitments to see if they lead us to that liberationist homiletic or if they stand in real contradiction to it.

For instance, a theology of ministry that suggests that the church's primary task in the world is to cultivate and nourish the spiritual lives of individual Christians would not serve us well in a preaching ministry seeking to empower the church as an agent of political and social change in human history. Likewise, a theology that worships and proclaims an other-worldly, wholly transcendent God, removed from this world and its pain and oppression, would not serve us well in a preaching ministry that seeks to alleviate that same oppression. A christology that suggests that Jesus uniquely and thoroughly exhausted the concept of Christ would not serve us well in a preaching ministry that seeks to empower and challenge individuals and whole communities to be the presence of the living Christ today. An ecclesiology that primarily understands the church's mission to be that of tending exclusively to the spiritual needs of its members would not serve us well in a preaching ministry that seeks to enable the people of God to be redemptive, salvific agents in the midst of human injustice and suffering.

One of the gifts that systematic theologians have given the church is the awareness that our theological beliefs and constructions need to have an internal consistency related to our ultimate commitments. For preachers seeking to be engaged in the work of liberation, we must examine and re-examine our theological beliefs in light of that work and that commitment. This theological examination is another discipline of a resurrection spirituality.

Considering this kind of theological examination around coherence and consistency, the following reflect what some of my own theology looks like as it directly flows from my own liberationist commitments.

Ministry

A theology of ministry is operative in a preacher's life whether that preacher is consciously aware of it or not, and it profoundly informs the craft and act of preaching. I understand ministry to be the liberating and salvific movement and activity of the people of God. I believe Christian ministry is the salvific and liberating movement and activity of the people of God, guided and shaped by the spirit of the Christ revealed to us in Jesus' life, death, and resurrection. This liberating and salvific activity has to do with eschatological vision and liberating praxis. As eschatological vision, the people of God seek to articulate, proclaim, and embody the hope of shalom, the promise of healing and restoration, the transforming reality of God's saving justice and love. As liberating praxis, the people of God place their lives in solidarity with the oppressed, transform structures of human injustice, confront and challenge powers of domination, and identify with and stand alongside the marginalized and disenfranchised of our world.

Because I embrace ministry as eschatological vision and liberating praxis, I clearly locate myself, as I have said already, within the larger theory and practice of liberation theology. This foundational commitment informs every aspect of my theological reflection and homiletical practice. My own theological method places scripture and tradition in dialogue with experience. In that dialogue there is a privileging of the oppressed and marginalized voices of our world. In the theological task of reflection and practice, voices of women, people of color, the poor, those with disabilities, gay and lesbian people, disempowered children, and older adults receive particular attention in both the deconstructive and constructive work of theology and ministry.

Central to the way I conceptualize Christian ministry as liberating and salvific activity are my understandings of God, christology, and ecclesiology.

God

I understand God to be sacred Spirit revealed as power and presence. I embrace Carter Heyward's understanding of God as the power of right relation, that which inspires, gives rise to, and creates mutuality among us; that which transforms, saves, and liberates.[2] I also understand God to be presence: that sacred dimension which exists within us, around us, and beyond us, sustaining and calling forth life among us. I do not believe God is primarily transcendent holy other but rather the matrix out of which creation takes shape and is sustained. I believe that God is a living, breathing part of all creation, yet more than we can name, understand, or fully know. I believe that God is in intimate relation to all creation, as creating, sustaining, empowering spirit. I do not believe in a God who is all-powerful and controlling; rather I believe that God's presence and expression is inextricably woven together with our human limitations and our human agency. This understanding of God will greatly influence how I see the presence and work of God when we move into a conversation about sin, evil, suffering, and injustice.

Christology

In the ministry and life of Jesus we have seen the possibility, the power, and the expression of redemptive, saving activity in the world. I believe that the power of God was incarnate in Jesus' liberating work in the world, and that the memory and vision of that work of liberation becomes normative for Christian lives. However, I do not believe that the historical Jesus exclusively embodies the Christ of faith. Wherever people live in the power of right relation or enter into radical acts of love or give witness to justice, there is the Christ. Wherever individuals are liberated, oppressive structures are transformed, and the power of evil is confronted, we stand in the presence of the Christ, God incarnate, God made manifest among us. We will explore this understanding of christology more fully when we move into a conversation about resurrection and what it means to be a people who embody resurrection power.

Ecclesiology

I believe that the Christian church is the community of faithful persons who understand their vocation in the world to be ministries of redemption and liberation. I stand close to countless liberation theologians who believe that there is often a vast difference between the institutional church, as we often know and experience it, and the liberating, resurrecting practices of the people of God. The institutional church has frequently stood on the side of social and economic power, which too often means it is an agent of death rather than life. Brazilian theologian Leonardo Boff states a simple, yet profound, ecclesiology when he says, "The Christian God is a God of life, and a God who calls the dead to life (cf. Rom. 4:17). There is no genuine testimonial to the Christian God where at least a minimal degree of life is not defended and fostered."[3]

Communities of faith struggling to participate in God's liberating activity of ministry often stand in stark contrast to the witness of institutional churches. If preachers and congregations were to accept Boff's challenge to be more fully those who give witness in the world to the God of life, then churches by definition would have to be involved in ministries of resistance against every force of death and violence.

Critically examining the coherence and consistency of our theological commitments to see if they can lead to a liberationist homiletic is the second spiritual and homiletical discipline of a resurrection spirituality.

> A third spiritual and homiletical discipline in a spirituality of resurrection is critical reflection upon every aspect of one's own theology in order to discern the ways it may perpetuate and undergird oppression.

Preachers engaged in a ministry of liberation commit themselves to rethinking the entire preaching task in relation to God language, biblical interpretation, christological doctrine, and all categories of one's own theology. This work can be excruciating; however, it is work that we must do for the preservation of our own spiritual and theological integrity and the preservation of our faith and belief in Christianity.

Theological assumptions that have often gone unquestioned must be critically re-evaluated on their impact upon the real lives of human beings in light of one's social analysis. We as preachers must examine ways that traditional theological constructs deny or romanticize forms of human suffering, serve to justify their existence, or focus only on the elite and privileged of this world. As preachers, we will engage in the difficult work of constructing new theological thinking that might help create a more just world.

In relation to sexism, for instance, some of this theological work might look like the following: (a) preachers developing a critical and constructive kind of biblical hermeneutics with a keen eye toward women's invisibility (Sarah and Hagar in the Sarah, Abraham, and Hagar story in Genesis), subtle and blatant expressions of violence against women found within texts (Jephthah's daughter in Judges), accounts of women's leadership (the Samaritan woman and her apostolic witness in John), and stories of women's strength and wisdom; or (b) a critical look at the ways our preaching ministries continue to uphold the privacy of the family at the expense of abused and battered women or the privacy of the family over the abuse of millions of children.

This kind of critical and deconstructive theological work must be done around every form of systemic oppression. It is a vast and challenging task, and one many preachers simply turn away from or ignore, but it is a crucial one nonetheless.

Dismantling oppressive theological constructs is as painful as proclaiming redemptive activity and liberation is celebrative. Both are needed from preachers who accept a ministry of resistance and a liberation homiletic and who are committed to a ministry that does not abandon life. Preachers do this theological work knowing that nothing less than people's lives are at stake. A resurrection spirituality will not let go of us and will not allow us to hide behind our comfortable theology at the expense of human life and human justice. We will return to this issue of deconstruction as we turn toward the homiletical task of resisting contemporary forms of crucifixion and inflicted violence.

> The fourth discipline connected to a spirituality of resurrection and a liberation homiletic has to do with the steps we take toward shaping our voices into voices of resistance and hope.

In my own work I have been searching for metaphors that adequately describe and inform the nature and shape of preaching as a ministry of resistance. In my second book, *Preaching as Weeping, Confession, and Resistance: Radical Responses to Radical Evil*,[4] I turned to *weeping, confession,* and *resistance* as metaphors that might create a distinctive homiletical methodology. How might preachers craft sermons that would passionately connect individuals and congregations to people who experience the pain and suffering of injustice and violence?

When this effectively happens in our preaching ministries, preaching becomes an act of weeping. Preaching as an act of weeping is about passionate connection and feeling, about moving closer to realities and people we would like to keep at a distance. It is about solidarity in the most profound sense of that word. Rita Nakashima Brock, in speaking about what enables us to engage in solidarity and what happens when we choose to be connected to the pain and oppression of others, says: "Through that healing energy we may choose, in solidarity with those who suffer, to give ourselves to their struggle, but that solidarity, when it emerges from our self-awareness, is not an act of self-sacrifice, but of self-possession and connection to others."[5] Preaching as an act of weeping is about self-possession and connection to others. It is an act that enlarges the self and moves whole religious communities closer to the salvific communities they say they are and want to be. It is an act of trying to move closer to a multitude of human and earthly realities that we may never know directly. It is an attempt to know and feel the injustices and exploitations we will never experience personally or collectively.

In an essay entitled "Theory as Liberatory Practice," bell hooks speaks about a similar starting place for the practice and art of teaching and the theory that undergirds it:

> It is not easy to name our pain, to theorize from that location. . . . I am grateful to the many women and men who dare to create theory from the location of pain and struggle, who courageously expose wounds to give us their experience to teach and guide, as a means to chart new theoretical journeys. Their work is liberatory.[6]

For preachers to theologize from the place of people's pain and oppression is equally courageous and necessary. This is not an act of despair; rather, it is an act of hope. It invites individuals and whole congregations to remember and honor all of creation, and it challenges religious people to renew their commitment to the liberatory work of the gospel. Speaking as an African American womanist theologian, M. Shawn Copeland describes the religious faithfulness of weeping as "Wading through Many Sorrows."[7] Choosing to preach from the location of people's pain is clearly a spiritual discipline undergirding a willingness, on the part of both preachers and congregations, to "wade through many sorrows." Taking this stance is a crucial step toward resistance preaching. It arises from a resurrection spirituality.

Confession, as another primary metaphor for a new homiletic, suggests that truth telling is absolutely essential in a preaching ministry that seeks to resist oppression and move toward liberation. If preaching takes as its starting point systemic evil and oppression, the preacher's honest social analysis may be indicative of how seriously that preacher embraces our human need for confession. When the truth of our human condition is proclaimed with courage, preaching becomes an act of confession. Nelson Mandela, in an endorsement of a collection of poems that seek to address social and political change, spoke about the power of poetry in a way that opens up the meaning of confessional truth telling. He said, "Poetry cannot block a bullet or still a *sjambok* (whip), but it can bear witness to brutality—thereby cultivating a flower in a graveyard."[8] Preaching as an act of confession, by the sheer force and possibility of its honesty, begins to cultivate life in the midst of a multitude of social and cultural graveyards.

It is clearly a spiritual discipline to engage in confessional truth telling and to move with our words and bodies into truths much of the privileged world would like to deny. Confession as "cultivating flowers in graveyards" is another essential step toward resistance preaching and is birthed and sustained out of a deep abiding resurrection spirituality.

Preaching as a ministry of resistance builds upon the foundations of weeping and confession. A preaching ministry that is deeply rooted in a commitment to bear up justice in the world in the face of what appears to be insurmountable evil is an act of resistance. It is crucial to name this kind of preaching *a ministry of resistance*, not a ministry of transformation. Though a transformed world is the ultimate hope that undergirds such a ministry, if preachers listen carefully to the oppressed voices surrounding them, they will discern that the language of survival, struggle, and resistance is what permeates these messages of indictment and hope, not the language of transformation. Transformative language assumes a certain measure of privilege and power that neither accurately describes nor reflects the lived realities of oppressed people. For preachers who minister from within communities struggling to sustain life, survival may be a central reality of human experience that is deeply acknowledged and understood. This is the starting place for relevant and vital preaching. For preachers who minister from within communities of social and economic privilege, struggle and survival become compelling categories of human experience that have the power to indict us and to reshape our proclamations.

Eleazar S. Fernandez, in his book *Toward a Theology of Struggle*, makes an important claim for the necessity of theological work that focuses on the struggle rather than the end result of liberation when he writes, "Liberation, as I perceive it, is still the direction of the theology of struggle, but the focus of the theology of struggle is on the struggle. The struggle is still long and protracted before the dawn of the new day may fully come."[9] Even though liberationist preaching as a ministry of resistance may ultimately move us toward liberation, it accents resistance because it takes the concrete reality of human struggle seriously. Whatever our social location, resistance language has a concreteness and a specificity that connects, enlivens, and fuels acts of justice.

Preaching as an act of resistance also does not focus its exclusive attention on suffering but urges us to join our own moral and ethical agency with the moral and ethical agency of those who are struggling against their own oppression. Ada María Isasi-Díaz, in an article about *mujerista* anthropology, describes the real lives of Latina women and the critical importance of focusing on their agency, their struggle, and their resistance, not just their suffering:

> I do not negate the reality of suffering in our lives, but I refuse to romanticize it, which I believe is what happens when one ascribes value to suffering in itself. . . . It is precisely when Hispanic Women's perspective of reality—including ourselves—is the lens used that *la lucha* [the struggle], not suffering, is seen as central to Latinas' humanity. Even in the moments of greatest suffering in our lives, if looked at from below and from within, the suffering is not what is most influential in determining how we act, talk, make decisions. Though Hispanic Women suffer racial/ethnic and sexist oppression and most of us also suffer poverty, we do not go about our *vida cotidiana*—our everyday life—thinking that we suffer but rather thinking how to struggle to survive, to live fully.[10]

A clear emphasis on our preaching as an act of resistance takes suffering and oppression seriously, but keeps a steady focus on the agency of all people struggling against it and the agency of many struggling to survive. It does not reduce people to victim status nor does it concentrate on suffering as an end in itself.

Speaking about preaching as a ministry of resistance rather than a ministry of transformation is not an assertion that minimizes or trivializes the craft and ministry of preaching. Naming preaching as a ministry of resistance attempts to honor the struggle that is involved in bringing about individual and collective change. Thus, it is an affirmation that makes hopeful and crucial claims of power. William Sloane Coffin says, "Hope resists, hopelessness adapts."[11] Resistance is an act of individual and collective hope. When preaching is a ministry of resistance, it participates in the shaping and forming of a people. A ministry of resistance informs and helps create whole communities of resistance.

Not only does poetry and poetic language enlarge our understanding of confession, the prophetic and transformational strategies of political poets can deepen our understanding of preaching as a courageous act of resistance as well. In a book about social and political resistance, Mary K. DeShazer attempts to articulate how poems actually participate in resistance. She offers a serious challenge to preachers about the intention, power, and courage of our words as well:

> First, they refuse the pretense of objectivity, instead asserting polemically the terms of their engagement with the topic at hand. In so doing, they claim as their own the task of historiographic reconstruction. Second, they violate poetic decorum in order to invite conflict and confrontation. They express anger stylistically via capital letters, exclamations, profanity, and arguments *ad hominem*; they hammer readers with aggressive catalogs, lengthy repetitions, and fierce rhetorical questions designed to evoke discomfort. For the reader's initial resistance will contribute ultimately to the success of the resistance poem. Finally, and simultaneously, they call forth from their audience an alternative complicity, a willingness to participate in a re-visionary project—ethical, political, literary—that could actually make a difference in the lives of the marginalized.[12]

Preachers need to evaluate the quality and power of their rhetorical and homiletical strategies to discern whether they could actually help reconstruct history and make a difference in the lives of those who are oppressed. Just as a poetics of resistance understands the necessity and importance of sometimes violating poetic decorum and using fierce rhetorical strategies in its justice work, preachers need to create new homiletical strategies that might violate homiletical decorum, yet be so truthful and courageous, they might actually call forth an "alternative complicity." Calling forth an alternative complicity is a discipline at the heart of a resurrection spirituality.

Recently, I encountered an article written by Pedro Casaldáliga, a Brazilian bishop, and José-María Vigil, a Nicaraguan priest, entitled "Ethical Indignation." In this article these two prophetic voices lift up with different language some of the same truths and commitments I have been trying to express with the metaphors of weeping, confession, and resistance. The authors believe that a theology of liberation has indeed produced a spirituality of liberation, and they are attempting to name some of the specific dimensions of that spirituality. One of the absolute center points of this spirituality is ethical indignation. They believe there are four basic elements involved in ethical indignation: perception of "basic reality," ethical indignation at this reality, perception of an inescapable demand, and our basic stance or option.[13]

Let me share a few of their words about these elements:

> In the first place, then, comes perception of "basic reality," what the situation is in its crudest form, what lies at its root. . . . [For Latin America this is] massive, engineered poverty on the continent.[14]

> On perceiving this basic reality we feel an "ethical indignation.". . . It is not an indignation that stems from any particular circumstance or ideology, but an indignation we know we feel by the mere fact of being human, so that if we did not feel it, we would not feel ourselves to be human. It is such an irresistible indignation that we cannot understand how other human beings can fail to feel it.[15]

> It is a radical indignation that brings with it an inescapable demand. It affects us, shakes us and moves us, imperatively. We feel questioned by it, in the depths of our being.[16]

> Now comes, unavoidably, the time to take a stance, to make a choice. . . . The stance taken might be a negative one: the opposite attitude to ethical indignation is hardness of heart, lack of sensitivity, indifference.[17]

> In this basic experience . . . [of perceiving reality—feeling ethical indignation at what we perceive, realizing there is an inescapable demand, and taking our stand on the side of the poor and oppressed and against injustice] we define ourselves. We define what our attitude is going to be in relation to absolute values. We establish what our cause is going to be, what meaning our lives are to have.[18]

The words of these two religious leaders are powerful and give us yet another way to think about a ministry of resistance and liberation. How will we cultivate and nurture ethical indignation and the demands it makes? How will we enable it in whole communities of faith, knowing that ethical indignation has everything to do with not abandoning life? I hear their words as those steeped in a resurrection spirituality.

Identifying the steps we must take in order to shape our preaching voices into voices of resistance and hope becomes the fourth discipline of a spirituality of resurrection. For me, many of those steps have centered around the metaphors of weeping, confession, and resistance. For some of us, the steps will lead toward cultivating ethical indignation.

⟩ A fifth spiritual and homiletical discipline of a spirituality of resurrection involves constantly listening to voices of critique and struggle outside one's cultural and social reality in order to expand and transform one's own homiletical agenda.

Voices of resistance and struggle can be found today within the academy of theological scholars. They can be found working among us in churches and communities immersed in everyday life. They are found as exiled voices driven from their own homeland. They are found moving about our city streets and in the intimacy of our living rooms. These voices of oppression and struggle are found in the midst of protest marches and presiding over the eucharist in mainline churches. Voices of resistance are appearing wherever people are violated and oppressed, wherever people hurt and suffer, and wherever people are longing for new life. These formative voices are claiming new truths, justice, and passionate life for individuals and whole communities. Any homiletic of resistance will seek to acknowledge and affirm the reality that countless preachers are being transformed by these radically diverse, sometimes indicting, voices.

Each of us will be uniquely changed by these voices depending upon our social location. How we experience a voice of resistance will depend on whether we reside within the community of resistance out of which that voice arises, or if we listen as an outsider. There are serious ethical issues involved as we listen to different voices and struggle to understand the impact of those voices upon our own preaching ministry and decide how we will draw upon those voices in the content of our sermons.

Appropriation is the act of using another's voice as if it is one's own. This is not an appropriate homiletical strategy. A more appropriate homiletical strategy might be to listen to voices different from our own in order to move more fully into the complex human distinctions that exist among us. For example, instead of using a Guatemalan poet's work as if we experienced what that artist describes and proclaims, we invite the poet to expose the classism and imperialism that permeate our own lives. Instead of white women preachers using African American women's theological critique and constructs as if we could speak *for* them or *with* them, we accept and receive their indictment of our own white racism. Listening to voices distinctly different from one's own in order to move more fully and faithfully into what those differences actually may mean for all of us is an act required of the preacher who would resist oppression and crucifixion. Seeking out these voices and attending to their messages, their worldviews, and their theologies is a crucial dimension of a resurrection spirituality.

Listening carefully to voices of critique and struggle outside one's cultural and social reality in order to expand and transform our homiletical agenda is the fifth spiritual and homiletical discipline of a spirituality of resurrection.

> The sixth spiritual and homiletical discipline of a spirituality of resurrection is to attend to the particularities of systemic oppression and to probe the connections between forms of oppression.

Because a preaching ministry of resistance assumes a very broad social and theological agenda, preachers will understand that no form of systemic oppression can be understood apart from all other forms of human oppression and injustice. As preachers we must examine economic realities and assumptions that pervade our common life. We must strive to understand the global impact of North American imperialism. Sermon illustrations will draw upon the distinctive worldviews and theological understandings of people with disabilities. The relational commitments and prophetic gender realities embodied in the lives of lesbians and gay men will be acknowledged and honored. White supremacy will be exposed as an ongoing expression of violence and evil in our contemporary lives. Preachers who engage in profound social analysis will be keenly aware that these realities are not disparate and unrelated realities but absolutely connected webs of oppression and injustice.

Preachers are invited and urged to see the interconnected reality of oppression in a multitude of ways. Iris Marion Young helpfully describes five dimensions that operate together in situations of oppression, yet each has its own distinctive character: exploitation, marginalization, powerlessness, cultural imperialism, and violence.

Exploitation refers to the systematic transfer of the benefit of one person's or group's work to the advantage of another. *Marginalization* is the unwillingness or inability of the economic system to use the capabilities of a person or group of persons. *Powerlessness* is the position of being the recipient of direction from others but being unable to give orders or exercise control over one's situation. *Cultural imperialism* is the universalization of one group's culture to the exclusion of all others. *Violence* names the dimension of institutionalized or socially permissible violence against persons or groups.[19]

Experiencing the oppression and the resultant suffering that comes with cultural imperialism is not the same as experiencing direct bodily violence. Exploitation of a whole community's resources and lifework is not the same as marginalization. These distinctions are very important and need to be honored in the preaching act.

In my book, *Preaching as Weeping, Confession, and Resistance*, I described four steps that preachers need to take as they move from social analysis to theological reflection, steps that also reveal at every turn the multiple ways these systems are interconnected and interrelated:

❖ Six forms of systemic oppression were specifically named: handicapism or ableism, ageism, sexism, hetero-sexism, white racism, and classism.

❖ I shared selected radicalizing moments I had experienced with each expression of evil. This step helped me clarify and understand how my own life had been challenged and changed by concrete encounters with dimensions of each form of oppression.

❖ Specific human faces of each form of oppression were identified, such as white racism and its economic violence and cultural imperialism; sexism with its resultant rape, battery, and incest; classism and the realities of homelessness, poverty, and unemployment. This is a crucial step in moving our preaching ministries from universal abstractions into the specificity and concreteness of human injustice.

❖ Finally, key theological affirmations that continue to justify and perpetuate each form of systemic oppression were identified and named. In some cases, new theological constructs were also articulated as examples of the kind of theological work needed to help eradicate each expression of oppression.[20]

Preaching as an act of resistance and liberation proclaims a vision that assumes the fundamental interrelatedness of all creation and seeks to nurture and inspire a deep sense of religious accountability. It is a kind of preaching that is predicated on the belief that social analysis is as crucial to the art of homiletics as theology and exegesis.

Attending to the particularities of systemic oppression and probing the connections between forms of oppression are both a part of the sixth spiritual and homiletical discipline in a spirituality of resurrection.

Summary

Awareness of the social context in which one is preaching and the social location of our own lives as preachers; an examination of the consistency of our theology as that which can lead us to salvific social and political acts; critical reflection upon every aspect of one's own theology in order to discern ways it may perpetuate and undergird oppression; taking the specific homiletical steps of weeping, confession, and resistance on the way to a preaching ministry of liberation; listening to voices of critique and struggle outside one's cultural and social reality in order to expand one's preaching agenda; and attending to the particularities and interconnections of systemic oppression: These spiritual and homiletical tasks and practices are crucial not just because they might enlighten, inspire, and enrich us, but because these practices and disciplines just might alleviate some small measure of human suffering and injustice. They are important because, in a world of unspeakable human indignities and immeasurable human violations, they might help us forge a collective alternative complicity that just might save us all and the earth on which we reside. These practices and disciplines just might help us refuse to abandon the basic life that lives at the center of the Christian faith.

Louis Evely reinterprets an ancient biblical teaching in a bold new way:

Fortunate are the poor in spirit. ∞

Fortunate are those who are willing
to let themselves be censured by the word of God,
to re-examine their views,
to believe they haven't yet understood a thing,
to be taken by surprise,
to have their mind changed,
to see their convictions,
their principles,
their tidy systems
and everything they took for granted
swept out from under them,
and to face the fact, once for all,
that there's no such thing as a matter of course
and that God can ask anything.[21]

SERMON:

"*!Es Posíble!*—It Is Possible!"

Preached at Re-Imagining 1993, Minneapolis
Read Matthew 15:21–28, Isaiah 55:1

I wish I could stand before you this day and tell you how inspiring I think this story of the Canaanite woman is: her strong presence, her persistent faith, her shameless audacity. I would like to be able to feel the full weight of joy as I experience this ancient story retold, celebrating her daughter's healing, smugly rejoicing in the truth that this woman expands Jesus' ministry, self understanding, and worldview as none other seems to—completely and thoroughly awed by the clarity of her mission. But as much as I can appreciate and celebrate this woman, I cannot celebrate this story. It is too filled with inequity, with dismissal, with demeaning power, and with dehumanization for me to be able to feel any real comfort or ease.

It is so much easier to speak about her bold voice than to sense the silent rejection by both the disciples and Jesus. It is so much more comforting to recognize her quick and persuasive insight than to feel this woman's kneeling. It is so much more uplifting and empowering to respect the faith of this woman bringing her daughter for healing than to acknowledge that this woman ultimately had to beg. I have always found this story angering and downright offensive.

The silencing of women's voices is oppressive. The dismissing of women's lived experience is dehumanizing. Forcing women to beg for the resources, power, healing, and care they need to sustain life for themselves and for their children is an act of violence. Perhaps some of us spiritualize the Canaanite woman's interaction with Jesus because it is less terrifying for us to encounter this narrative as one of faith and hope than to face this woman's story as one of violence and survival. Great is her faith and great is the oppression.

"Ho, everyone who thirsts, come to the water; and you that have no money, come, buy and eat! Come, buy wine and milk without money and without price."

I fear that this woman is like so many women throughout the ages: a

23

courageous survivor, a powerful moral agent who is determined to find water, wine, and milk, and does, but with great cost and at a very high price.

The commentators idealize her saying she shocks, shames, and charms us to imitate her bold and persistent faith. Maybe this woman does not want to shock or shame or charm anyone. Perhaps this woman simply wants access to those things that make for fullness of life. Perhaps she wants the marginalization of her daughter to stop. Perhaps she wants her ethnicity to be respected and honored. Perhaps she wants men to treat her with full human regard.

I have often wondered, and I invite us all to wonder, what this woman might be saying to her friends as she leaves this scene having shouted for help and initially been ignored, having knelt down on her knees before this powerful man and having spoken the words, "Yes, Lord, yet even the dogs eat the crumbs that fall from their master's table." Crumbs are a far cry from abundant water, wine, and milk without price.

Last May I was in Guatemala with two of my colleagues from United Seminary. We were sitting in a small open-air restaurant one evening in Chichicastenango reflecting on our day. It was dusk. People were busily removing the last visible signs of the day's market. While we were absorbed in conversation, a small boy, maybe six or seven years old, came up to me and began to tug at my shirt sleeve asking me for money.

I ignored him for a while and then finally I said in my blunt and unpolished Spanish, "*No es posíble*" ("It is not possible"). He kept tugging and I repeated at least twice more, "*No es posíble*." Finally, I looked him in the eye. He engaged me squarely back and simply said, "*Es posíble*" ("It *is* possible"). I was totally undone. I reached in my pocket, gave him some money, and he was on his way.

Change from the pockets of the rich must feel like crumbs. It surely is not water, wine, and milk at no price.

There is something frighteningly similar about these two stories. If we want to be casually inspired by them, we will speak about the faith of this bold Canaanite woman and the persistence of this small Guatemalan child. If we want to be changed by them, we will speak about the poverty, the racism, the power, the need, and the oppression that forces most of the people of the globe to beg for food, for human dignity, for equal honoring, for life. The realities of many of our lives directly force others to beg for what is needed. I cannot help wondering if Jesus felt this horrible truth as much as I did that evening in Chichicastenango.

This small Guatemalan boy has been teaching me for months now that there is a vast difference between what we are able to do and what we are unwilling to do. It would have been far more honest to have said, "I do not want to share my money with you" or "I am not willing to share my money with you." What I spoke was an illusion and a lie. The truth was never that I was not able. The truth was never that it was not possible.

Re-imagining is about discerning and celebrating what is possible: the possibility of a world where no one has the power to dismiss, no one sits while others kneel, no community eats exclusively from the table. It is about the possibility of a world where all people are heard, where resources for life are distributed equitably, where all people have access to what is on the table, and where no one eats crumbs. It is about water running freely, wine poured out extravagantly, milk flowing endlessly. Re-imagining is about discovering what we can create and shape together, and it is about holding one another accountable in every conceivable way with the words and praxis of "*Es posible.*" "It is possible."

But even to say these words is too easy. The work of re-imagining is not the same work for each of us. For some of us it will be the work of channeling our influence; for others of us it is work that will save the lives of our family members. Some of us will be compelled to relinquish privilege; others of us will feel forced to pick up guns to defend our villages. It is all important work, crucial work, necessary work, even though some of the shocking and confronting differences in urgency and daily survival must never cease to move us into more radical action in the world.

The songs, the poetry, the art, and the verse that emerge from the lived realities of our lives reveal in a poignant and wonderful way the different work that must be engaged in by each one of us and the necessity of having powerful strong images to remind us of that work. In a song entitled "Cradle of Dawn," Libby Roderick sings to a person halfway around the world about the struggle they are both engaged in for justice and for life. At one point she sings:

> The forces facing us are terrible indeed
> My hope may flicker in the night
> But in the morning I will plant another seed
> And while you sleep it seeks the light

There are no promises that we will see the day
The dreams we live for will succeed
But I can promise you that halfway round the world
I'll hold the light up while you sleep.[22]

In this global gathering let us vow to hold the beacon of justice up wherever we live, wherever we work, wherever we share life in community, and let us never cease from planting one seed of life after another.

Alongside of Libby Roderick's passionate voice, we hear, we feel, Julia Esquivel's compelling and urgent challenge to us also:

I am no longer afraid of death,
   I know well
   its dark and cold corridors
   leading to life.

I am afraid rather of that life
   which does not come out of death
   which cramps our hands
   and slows our march

I am afraid of my fear
   and even more of the fear of others,
   who do not know where they are going,
   who continue clinging
   to what they consider to be life
   which we know to be death![23]

In this global gathering let us vow to walk some of the dark and cold corridors of death that lead to life, no matter what our fears may be, and no matter how much some of our privilege might otherwise protect us from such reality. Let us plant seeds and let us walk cold corridors, let us hold up the light while another sleeps, and let us stop clinging to death.

Re-imagining is not just about rejoicing in human difference, experiencing inclusive liturgies, listening to visionary theological voices and building isolated and removed pockets of human community. Re-imagining is about building a world where the elite and privileged must face their own complicity in the oppression of others, oppression that is constant and death dealing.

Re-imagining is about building a world where the poor, the powerless, the marginalized seize the power to shape their own destinies.

It is about having land to farm, water to drink, food to eat, work that instills dignity, and basic health care for all. Water must flow more easily and fully because we have been here. Wine must pour forth more equitably because we have been here. And milk must flow to the ends of the earth.

To do this work we must be able to imagine what is possible. We must be willing to move into the fear of human difference. We must be willing to face the claims that will be made upon our voices, our writing, our money, our time, our safety, our relationships, our lives.

At the end of September, I went to Los Angeles for an urban immersion experience with other colleagues from around the country who are a part of the Association of Practical Theology. The entire weekend was stretching and challenging, yet one encounter remains in my mind and heart in a distinct way. Here we sit, fifteen practical theologians who pride ourselves somewhat in the fact that we work very hard to bring theory and practice together in the kind of theological education that will equip people for effective ministry in the world. Sitting as a part of our circle are Veronica and Vicki. They are social workers who walk the streets of L.A. on a daily basis searching for and seeking out women who are at high risk of contracting AIDS. Earlier in their lives they both have been drug users and street dwellers. With absolute clarity, Vicki says, "Every five minutes someone is infected, every fifteen minutes someone dies. AIDS is not a moral issue, it is a health issue."

The two women describe their work with passion and profound integrity. At one point Vicki says, "Each day we go in pairs. We wear our badges, pick up our outreach bags filled with condoms and bleach to clean needles, and we go looking for women."

After some time, one of our group, who can stand it no longer, says, "Where I teach, and where I live my life, how people contract AIDS would certainly be a moral issue. Would you say more?" Vicki simply replies, "AIDS is not a moral issue, it is a health issue."

Frustrated and somewhat angry, the man in our group comes back two more times, until finally Vicki says, "If you feel the need to dwell on the moral question, and to debate the issue, that is where you must be. For us, AIDS is not a moral issue, it is a health issue, and people are dying."

Water, wine, and milk gush forth in the mission, the urgency, the unswerving commitment of these two women. There is a vast difference between participating in academic discussions and distributing outreach bags of condoms and bleach.

Transformational work is not about remaining still and defending ourselves against the evil that surrounds us, but it is a movement into it, and through it, with speech and presence and action. It is about gathering up our outreach bags with whatever it takes to get the job done. It is work that places our lives in fundamentally new places, sometimes positioning our passions and our bodies in dark and cold corridors that feel like death.

In our worship book for this conference, re-imagining is described as that which sustains our common vocation of transformation. Many are the dimensions of this struggle. Doing what must be done, what is possible to do, is a courageous act. This endless work is a dance of fire, passion, and persistence.

For some of us it is a dance; for others a slow but steady walk. For yet others of us it will be a dance done from wheelchairs and hospital beds with cane in hand and with faltering step, but it will be done.

Sylvia Dunstan reminds us in the hymn, "Bless Now, O God, the Journey," that we are sojourners and pilgrims who share a winding way and whose hope burns through the terror.[24]

It is the hope and terror of shaping a world where we understand this truth with absolute clarity. As we re-imagine God, Jesus, creation, church, sexuality, word, ethics, ministry, the worshiping community, work, the arts, we are in fact imagining our way into a world where the bodies of our daughters, our mothers, our sisters, and our lovers will be cherished; women, children, men will preserve the earth and live reverently with all its creatures; cultural differences will be protected and ethnic heritage honored; women will be able to embrace each other as lovers feeling beautiful and unafraid; the world's hungry will have enough to eat; people with disabilities will have equal and total access to buildings, work, sexuality, relational dignity; the young will be valued for their wisdom and their innocence, and the old will be treasured for their passion and their guidance. It is a winding way. It is a way filled with hope burning through the terror.

As the water and wine and milk of our work flow forth, there will be no more begging, no more Guatemalan children begging, no more Canaanite women begging, no more crumbs, and no more begging.

Sweet Honey In The Rock sings a paraphrased version of a quote that has inspired the United Mine Workers of America in their struggle for justice and just may be a fitting challenge to the work that faces us ahead.

Step by step the longest march can be won, can be won,
Many stones can form an arch, singly none, singly none,
And by union what we will can be accomplished still,
Drops of water turn a mill, singly none, singly none.[25]

Drop by drop, step by step, and as we go this unnamed Canaanite woman
winds the road with us and shouts for us to move quickly.

3

Drinking Pain and Resisting Crucifixions

Today, in the face of every kind of pervasive violence that touches and affects us all, and in the face of every conceivable crucifixion, what does effective and faithful liberation preaching look like? To answer this question, preachers must begin with the concrete, lived realities of our homes, our neighborhoods, our countries, and our globe. It is never that the Bible, tradition, and our particular faith communities are unimportant; they simply must not always be the primary and exclusive starting points for our theology and preaching in a day of such social and political urgency.

The Reality of Crucifixion

With this commitment to the concrete, lived realities of people's lives, let us turn to a few of what could be an endless procession of voices and images. If we allow, these voices and concrete images immerse us within the material world of suffering and oppression and quickly and powerfully move us into the human reality of contemporary crucifixions:

> During the summer of the 1965 drought I was drawn one day by curiosity to the jail cell of a young woman from an outlying rural area who had just been apprehended for the murder of her infant son and her one-year-old daughter. The infant had been smothered, and the little girl had been hacked with a machete. Rosa, the mother, became for a brief period a central attraction in Bom Jesús, as both rich and poor passed by her barred window which opened to a side street, to rain down invectives on her head: "Animal," she was called, "unnatural creature," "shameless woman." Face to face with the withdrawn and timid slip of a girl (she seemed barely a teenager), I made myself bold enough to ask the obvious: "Why did you do it?" She replied as she must have for the hundredth time, "To stop them from crying for milk."[1]

> Last spring, a young man named Sig died. He was the twenty-four-year-old son of a United Methodist minister. Sig was born with a form of epilepsy that was never totally controlled but was being managed

by medication. He became involved in a church (not United Methodist) that welcomed him warmly and included him in their fellowship. But this church preached that if he just had enough faith, he would be *healed* of his epilepsy. Encouraged to prove just how much faith he had, Sig stopped taking his medication. Soon afterward, he suffered a seizure and died.[2]

Before Tim's next visit home, for his sister's sweet sixteen party, his parents had questioned his brother and sister and concluded that they had a "fag in the family" after all. When he appeared at the party, his father remarked: "Son if you want to be queer as a three-dollar bill, that's your business." Tim walked away without saying a word. Then his mother approached him. She put her arm around his shoulders. Tim took this to mean that she was going to accept him. "Tim," she said, "I've made only one mistake in my life." Tim asked her what she meant. "Twenty-two years ago," she said, "I should have had an abortion." Since then, Tim's mother has taken to telling neighbors and friends that he is dead. And Tim's father speaks to him as if he were a complete stranger when Tim calls to speak to his sister or brother.[3]

Don't pity the infants who died here on the Alto do Cruzeiro. Don't waste your tears on them. Pity us instead. Weep for their mothers who are condemned to live.[4]

These are contemporary faces of oppression and crucifixion. There are many people in our world who feel "condemned to live," and so many voices of the Christian church in North America are strangely silent in the face of such realities. For us to be able to fully name present-day resurrection experiences, we must first tend to the crosses that crucify people, crucifixions that fundamentally rob people of life.

The Prophetic Preacher: Denunciation and Proclamation
The Brazilian liberation theologian Leonardo Boff puts the challenge before us clearly:

It means that we must become prophets. . . . Prophets live two radical fidelities at once. One is to God, in whose name they proclaim and denounce. The other is to the people, the poor, on whose behalf they raise their voices and utter their cry.[5]

I want to lift up a few of the many tasks that I believe are crucial in a preaching ministry that seeks to proclaim and denounce, a preaching ministry that seeks to resist crucifixion.

The first task of a preaching ministry that seeks to resist crucifixions is that preachers must become more adept in distinguishing the vast differences between kinds of human suffering.

Jon Sobrino reminds us of what we would like to deny and forget: "To die crucified does not mean simply to die but to be put to death."[6] Preachers who would resist injustice and crucifixions must first be willing to acknowledge the multitudes of people in this world who do not simply die but are put to death by the forces of systemic oppression.

Not all suffering is the same. There is suffering that comes as a result of the natural flow of life and death, and then there is human suffering that is inflicted. When a human being loses a loved one it is a time of suffering and grief, yet this is a very different kind of suffering than the intentional annihilation of whole villages in Guatemala. Also, there is suffering that people choose as they stand in solidarity with those who suffer and who are oppressed, and there is suffering that is systematically intended for particular groups and individuals. Marie Fortune describes this as the difference between voluntary and involuntary suffering.[7] Preachers must begin to nuance with concreteness and truthfulness the worlds of difference between various kinds of human suffering.

Far too often we hear preachers simply pronounce that all human beings suffer. People in Halifax suffer. People in South Africa suffer. People in our cities suffer. People in rural villages suffer. The moment we make generalizations about something as critical as human suffering, we have masked the horrors of inflicted suffering. This kind of generalization will not help the Christian church discern how to effectively respond to distinct and vastly different kinds of human suffering. This kind of generalization also leads us to believe that human suffering of every kind is simply the nature of things and an inevitable part of human reality. Social, political, and ecclesiastical resistance seldom flows from this kind of generalization.

What kinds of human suffering are we most likely to address in our preaching? Which forms and expressions of human suffering tend to claim our attention and our analysis? About which forms of human suffering do we find ourselves strangely silent?

In trying to clarify the origins of human suffering, Christian preachers continue to name the problem most often in terms of individual human sinfulness rather than historical, systemic oppression. In trying to find some meaningful way to co-exist with suffering, countless preachers continue to suggest that suffering will strengthen character and deepen the spirit of those who accept it, and that those who endure it well are the most faithful and saintly. In trying to move beyond suffering, many preachers would rather linger in the realm of life after death for individuals, or focus on the reign of God as eschatological hope, than confront and challenge congregations to be the creators of the reign of God as historical reality now.

Relevant and pastorally sensitive preaching will always be faced with the challenge of responding to many different faces of human suffering, for they surround us in our own congregations, neighborhoods, and world. Faithful preaching must try to look at all the ways human beings respond to those experiences of suffering. However, after centuries of the Christian church's giving priority voice to forms of individual suffering, it seems essential that preachers begin to speak out against historical and systemic forms of human suffering in our proclamations. Often these forms of suffering are the very kinds of suffering that the Christian church ignores, denies, or participates in as an agent of oppression. I will continue to look at crucifixion in this chapter, and resurrection in chapters four and five, from within this perspective.

Not only is there the theological and homiletical work of differentiating types of suffering, there are also denouncements and proclamations to be made about suffering. These might lead us a little closer to preaching ministries that resist crucifixions. These statements pertain to inflicted, unjust, and unnecessary suffering.

Denunciations

❖ Inflicted suffering is not redemptive; it is pain, horror, and degradation. Various ways human beings respond to suffering may have elements of redemptive power and possibility within them, but those redemptive responses to suffering are distinct from the suffering itself.

❖ Inflicted suffering and the endurance of pain should never be preached or encouraged as ends in themselves. Sometimes people must endure pain in order to survive; sometimes people endure pain on behalf of some greater good; sometimes people endure pain on the way toward individual and social transformation. Survival, a greater good, or individual and social transformation are the ends, not the suffering and the endurance of pain.

❖ God does not will or desire inflicted suffering; rather, human beings create and sustain inflicted suffering and injustice.

❖ Eschatological (i.e. future or otherworldly) responses to inflicted suffering are not enough. These responses often serve to justify passivity and indifference in relation to the horrors of people's present lives.

❖ Individual sin as the primary explanation for inflicted suffering is inadequate and inaccurate and falsely leads us to believe that individual morality will alleviate the magnitude of inflicted suffering that exists worldwide.

Proclamations

❖ Inflicted, involuntary suffering must be struggled against and resisted in every way possible, not just endured.

❖ Historical, systemic injustice and suffering are not inevitable; they can be dismantled and resisted.

❖ There is a vast difference between kinds of human suffering, and those differences can and must be named, understood, and responded to concretely.

❖ Instead of unnecessary and unjust suffering, God desires justice and fullness of life for every creature.

❖ The reign of God, the new community, the transformed world, can be created and built in historical time and space.

❖ The actions human beings take to resist inflicted suffering and to stop injustice have redemptive, saving power.

Patricia Wismer pushes us to see why these denouncements and proclamations about suffering are so crucial:

> An omnipotent God who sends, allows, or permits suffering for whatever reason . . . (as a spur to growth, as a punishment for sin, as a test of our faith, as a means of redeeming others, as a way of increasing the fullness of life, etc.) still looks remarkably like a sadist if we take off our theological spectacles and see what is actually before our eyes.[8]

Not only must human beings become more accountable for the ravages of inflicted suffering, but the very nature and activity of God is at stake in how we understand and interpret suffering. May we turn from all kinds of preaching that make God a punitive sadist. May we have the courage to take off our theological spectacles and see what is actually happening when real human beings suffer injustice. May our denunciations and proclamations about inflicted human suffering be bold and prophetic.

> The second task of a preaching ministry that seeks to resist
> crucifixions is that we as preachers must ask ourselves what
> religious and theological questions will lead us to respond with
> resistance and liberatory action and what religious questions
> immerse us in abstractions and denial.

I have come to believe that the theodicy question (i.e., How can a good
and loving God allow human suffering?) is not the kind of question
that will lead us to action and response. This question keeps us looking
beyond ourselves to something or someone who will be more accountable, more ethically active, more faithful and more responsive than we
ourselves are willing to be. It keeps us asking, *Who will save us? Who
will change all that needs changing, preserve all that needs preserving,
transform all the problems, sustain all the good? Who will save us?* These
questions, and all the other questions that swirl around theodicy,
seldom prompt and inspire people of faith to engage in redemptive,
saving acts. We must ask ourselves as preachers, *What kind of religious
and theological questions are we willing to ask? And what are the
questions that will lead us to acts of justice and liberation?*

It will always be important for people of faith to ask, *Where is God?*
Even more importantly, our world needs questions that will move and
convert people, questions that will change human lives.

In our preaching, when will we ask what we must do to change an
economic system that will not allow family farms to survive instead of
always asking why the family farmer is not a success?

When will members of the Christian church ask what exactly must
we all do together to stop AIDS instead of always asking who are the
kind of people who get AIDS?

When will we as religious people ask how we are complicit in the
despair that leads to violence in our cities instead of always asking why
are there not more police and more arrests?

When will our congregations ask why was it ever permissible or
acceptable to have offices, churches, parks, schools, restrooms, sidewalks
inaccessible to persons with disabilities instead of always asking what
will it cost us to make our common life inclusive?

These kinds of questions about the nature of the church and the
nature of human reality and justice do not keep us looking beyond
ourselves, nor do these questions lead us to blame those who experience injustice, violence, and crucifixions. These questions are
exposing, indicting, and so truthful that when preachers and congrega-

tions dare to ask them, possibilities for life open up for all. These are
the kinds of questions that urge us to act ethically, to respond compas-
sionately in ways never imagined, and to spend our lives in ways that
make some real difference. Asking, *Why does God allow suffering?* will
always stand in stark contrast to the words and challenge of Ignácio
Ellacuria:

> I want you to set your eyes and your hearts on these peoples who are
> suffering so much—some from poverty and hunger, others from
> oppression and repression. Ask yourselves: what have I done to
> crucify them? What do I do to uncrucify them? What must I do for
> this people to rise again?[9]

Are preachers and whole congregations courageous enough to ask, *What
have we done to crucify people, what must we do to uncrucify people, and
how will our actions and our lives help people rise again?*

> A third task for a preaching ministry that seeks to resist crucifix-
> ions involves the preacher moving from an emphasis on
> christology to a focus on christo-praxis.

This task is intricately related to the second task, for it also has to do
with the kind of questions we spend our time asking and addressing.
Christology is a theological concept that largely focuses on questions of
Jesus' identity and being. Questions at the heart of christology involve
who Jesus was as both divine and human person or what kind of
differences and distinctions there are between the historical Jesus and
the Christ of faith. Christo-praxis involves the theological task of
discerning what it means for Christian people to actually *be* a christic
presence in the world. Carter Heyward names the challenge of moving
toward questions of christo-praxis well:

> It is my thesis here that the historical doctrinal pull between Jesus of
> Nazareth and Jesus Christ, the human Jesus and his divine meaning,
> is no longer, if it ever was, a place of creative christological inquiry.
> Worse, it is a distraction from the daily praxis of liberation, which is
> the root and purpose of Christian faith.[10]

In shifting from a focus on christology to christo-praxis, two
challenges face us. The first part of this movement involves the
systematic critique of every aspect of sacrificial theology that has formed
a Christian faith which idealizes crucifixions, suffering, and crosses.
A key theological task before North American Christian preachers of
privilege today is a serious and relentless critique, or deconstruction, of
theologies of the cross that have masked the horrors of human

suffering, justified oppressive crucifixions, and celebrated sacrifice as an end in itself. Although this critique is only the beginning step in moving us closer to a homiletic that clearly resists crucifixions, it is a step that is absolutely crucial. Ultimately, we need sermons that enable Christian people to understand that the Christian mandate to "take up one's cross" is a mandate to be in solidarity with the crucified of history and ultimately involves moving against those crosses. Taking up a cross does not have to idealize human sacrifice and suffering; rather, it can point to all those concrete ways human beings live in solidarity with those who are oppressed and are willing to do whatever is necessary to stop inflicted suffering. More will be said about this specifically when we get to the section on the cross.

Preachers are key religious interpreters who can begin to help religious communities identify and condemn the contemporary crucifixions of our day. This involves a refusal to romanticize, justify, or rationalize them theologically. This critical work also involves challenging whole communities to harness their collective power in efforts to stop them.

A second part of the movement from christology to christo-praxis involves identifying, naming, and participating in those activities in life that are truly redemptive. Heyward describes this part of the work when she says, "In this praxis theological knowing would cease to be a matter of discovering *the* Christ and would become instead a matter of generating together images of what is redemptive or liberating in particular situations."[11]

Preachers and whole congregations need to discover and generate together images and actions that are redemptive with the same kind of specificity and concreteness as the homiletical task of nuancing our analysis of human suffering. Moving from christology to christo-praxis means we must ask these kinds of questions:

❖ What does redemptive activity look like in the face of violence against women? One image, largely generated by the battered women's movement outside the church, is "breaking silence." Breaking silence is one expression of redemptive activity in response to violence against women. Breaking the silence that surrounds violence against women is the first step in a movement toward ending that same violence.

❖ What does redemptive activity look like in the face of ableism and the specific issue of physical access? Perhaps architectural changes are one expression of redemptive activity and christo-praxis. Providing sign-language interpreters in all of our churches might be another expression of the daily praxis of liberation.

❖ What does redemptive christo-praxis look like in the face of an unprecedented percentage of gay and lesbian teenagers killing themselves? Perhaps redemptive christo-praxis might look like church communities assisting schools where support groups for gay and lesbian teenagers exist or advocating for the creation of such groups. Perhaps christo-praxis might look like preachers challenging the Christian church and its continual use of scriptural texts that silence, judge, and condemn lesbian and gay people.

❖ What does redemptive christo-praxis look like in relation to the violence of United States imperialism? Perhaps redemptive christo-praxis looks like a church community buying acres of land from corporate landowners in a small village in Guatemala, only to turn the property deeds over to the people of that village. It looks like a church community that protests military schools and bases in the United States where Central American military officers are trained in techniques of terrorism and torture.

These are only a few of the images and actions that need to be generated by Christian communities in an effort to move toward the kind of action in the world that has redemptive, saving power. The church and Christian preachers in particular need also to humbly acknowledge that those images and actions are created and sustained by social agencies and services more than they are created and generated by the church.

> A fourth task for a preaching ministry that seeks to resist crucifixion is that preachers need to take up survival as a critical theological and ethical issue for preaching.

Many Euro-American and Canadian preachers, particularly those of us who are economically privileged, find it nearly impossible to understand or comprehend the fundamental issue of survival that permeates and forms the social reality of many people throughout the world. If white preachers of privilege cannot begin to grasp more fully this issue of survival, we will never be able to understand the ultimate dividing lines and violent implications of white supremacy, cultural and economic imperialism, militarism, and class oppression that influence all of our lives. Survival is a profound religious and theological category for contemporary preaching. Survival has everything to do with crucifixions, injustice, and oppression.

A part of the task for preachers dealing with survival as a theological and ethical issue is to understand that people who are struggling to survive can never be simply reduced to the status of victim. To suggest that the poor, those suffering under the oppression of white racism, sexism, heterosexism, ageism, or ableism, are only victims and not agents of life is to perpetuate another kind of violence on a people. In a book entitled *Death Without Weeping: The Violence of Everyday Life in Brazil*, anthropologist Nancy Scheper-Hughes writes strong words about the essential nature of the task of naming the oppression while also naming the powerful agency of a people. She says these words about the people in Brazil she had studied and shared life with for years:

> In these pages I have tried to argue a middle ground, one that acknowledges the destructive signature of poverty and oppression on the individual and the social bodies, for Freire's "culture of silence" is recognizable on the Alto do Cruzeiro, but one that also acknowledges the creative, if often contradictory, means the people of the Alto use to stay alive and even to thrive with their wit and their wits intact. The goal of the *moradores* of the Alto do Cruzeiro is not *resistance* but simply *existence*. And in the context of these besieged lives I find human resilience enough to celebrate with them, joyfully and hopefully, if always tentatively.[12]

When she speaks of "middle ground" in her own work, she is trying to hold two distinct realities of the people in tension: the reality of daily survival and the reality of human resiliency and agency. She portrays them clearly as subjects, not objects. She honors their resistance at moments and also acknowledges that most of what they must do is simply work to exist, to survive.

Over a decade ago, Katie Cannon, in *Black Womanist Ethics*, urged us to see that black women make their moral and ethical decisions out of an environment of survival, not freedom. She confronted the theological world with the notion that freedom as the starting point of ethical decision making is a white, dominant construct having little relevance for black women's lives and only serves to minimize, trivialize, and reduce the real moral and ethical agency of black women's lives.[13] To understand the moral agency of black women's lives, one would need to fully understand the concrete expressions of *invisible dignity, quiet grace,* and *unshouted courage.*[14] I can only suppose that Cannon's ethical and moral assertions are known to many African American women preachers and assumed as a part of the foundational fabric of daily life. For white preachers who have been profoundly influenced by dominant thinking that idealizes personal freedom as the source of human action and choice, Cannon's words provide a crucial challenge. A part of Cannon's challenge to the preacher is to stop making universalizing ethical statements and to start deepening the ways we contextualize issues of moral and ethical agency and action.

In a similar radical vein, Delores Williams, in *Sisters in the Wilderness: The Challenge of Womanist God-Talk,* shifts our biblical and theological thinking. With a clear and persistent focus on the Egyptian slave woman Hagar, whose oppression and moral agency are recorded in Genesis, Williams invites us into a multilayered conversion experience. She challenges all of us who use liberation language and analyze our social, political, and ecclesiastical lives out of liberation categories, suggesting that those liberation categories and constructs are inadequate. "The Hagar-Sarah texts in Genesis and Galatians, however, demonstrate that the oppressed and abused do not always experience God's liberating power," she writes.[15] Williams refuses to be convinced that Hagar's story is one of liberation and presses us to consider it a story of survival. Hagar and African American women who have endured after her have lived their lives much more out of a survival/quality-of-life ethic than out of a liberationist ethical position.[16] At the very least, she is suggesting that there is a fundamental tension between liberation ethics and survival/quality-of-life ethics. In response to the ethical shift she suggests, she invites us to reconsider the nature of God and God's saving activity, the nature of human existence, and the nature of moral and ethical activity. She finally suggests that perhaps *wilderness* is a more appropriate description of the lived experience of African American women, and the locus of God's activity, than Exodus.[17]

Any preacher today needs to take seriously the voices of African American womanist theologians. These womanist theologians raise critical issues for preaching within the African American church experience, and they demand biblical and theological transformation from those of us who are listening from the outside. Not only are they suggesting that we take survival as a starting point for theology and preaching seriously, they promise to shift all our ethical categories and understandings and deepen and change our assertions about God's saving, redemptive activity. Shifting from liberation to wilderness as a locus of God's presence and a primary place of human moral agency is a monumental challenge to the language and theology of preaching, including liberationist preaching. Cannon and Williams remind us that it is not enough to use liberationist language in addressing the complexities of injustice and oppression. We must push even deeper into language of survival, struggle, and wilderness.

Other women speak about survival in ways that are instructive for our theological and homiletical lives. Donna Kate Rushin describes the embodied marks of racism and survival on her own life as a woman of color as "this bridge called my back."[18] Gloria Anzaldúa describes her life as lesbian and Chicana as living in the "borderlands."[19] She says, "Tension grips the inhabitants of the borderlands like a virus. Ambivalence and unrest reside there and death is no stranger."[20] Chung Hyun Kyung speaks about Asian women's lived experience in this way: "Colonialism, neo-colonialism, militarism, and dictatorship are everyday reality for most Asian women. . . . They create food for life out of nothing. Their bodies take and carry all the burdens for survival."[21]

If we allow ourselves to encounter all these passionate voices: their critiques, their visions, their distinctive world views, their theological constructions, and their lived faithfulness, our preaching ministries will change. Many of these voices speak from within a collective, community identity that gives rise to a radically different context for preaching than does a middle-class Euro-American or Euro-Canadian context of comfortable privilege and isolated individualism. There are indeed holy places of difference among us that both challenge and terrify any conscientious preacher. A preaching ministry of resistance urges us to listen well to these voices of survival and then to speak and act boldly.

> A fifth task for a preaching ministry seeking to resist crucifixions is for preachers to reconstruct and expand our understandings of sin and evil.

In 1960, Valerie Saiving wrote an article titled "The Human Situation: A Feminine View." This article appeared to be the first time that traditional understandings of sin were critically identified as exclusive reflections of white, male experience. Saiving asserted a woman's insights about sin:

> The temptations of woman *as woman* are not the same as the temptations of man *as man*, and the specifically feminine forms of

sin . . . have a quality which can never be encompassed by such terms
as "pride" and "will to power." They are better suggested by such terms
as triviality, distractibility, and diffuseness; lack of an organizing
center or focus; dependence on others for one's self-definition;
tolerance at the expense of standards of excellence . . . in short,
underdevelopment or negation of the self.[22]

In the past three decades, numbers of women theologians have added
their voices to the discussion of sin and evil, and several points of
similarity have surfaced in the midst of ever-increasing diversity: (a)
Most feminist and African American womanist women are highly
suspicious and critical of individualistic, privatized understandings of
human immorality/morality that have so dominated discussions about
sin; (b) There has been a persistent shift from sin and evil as being
defined as pride, disobedience, idolatry, and alienation to sin and evil
as violation of right relation (Carter Heyward), a sign of our
brokenheartedness (Rita Nakashima Brock), a betrayal of trust (Mary
Potter Engel), the reign of injustice (Karen Lebacqz), the consequence
of disparities of power (Beverly Wildung Harrison), and as tyrannical
systems of oppression (Katie Geneva Cannon); (c) Many feminist and
womanist writers push beyond the individualism of sin by concentrat-
ing their primary work on naming and defining the more corporate,
systemic reality of evil; and (d) Increasing care has been given to
naming the social location of the theologian and the specific human
contexts that give rise to every particular and nuanced expression of
evil or sin.

Just as other theological categories must be understood in relation
to context and the social location of the theologian, preacher, or person
of faith, so the same is true for sin. Sin and evil may be understood in
radically different ways within distinct and different communities.

A very helpful example of the contextualizing of sin can be found in
Susan Thistlethwaite's book, *Sex, Race, and God*. In this very provoca-
tive volume, Thistlethwaite attempts to bring black and white women
into serious dialogue about their vast differences. On the book flap she
poses a question that informs the entire project: "What happens when
the differences between black and white women become the starting
point for white feminist theology?" Remaining true to particularity,
Thistlethwaite attempts to name sin as it specifically relates to white
women in a white supremacist culture. She confronts white women with
a particular view of our own sinfulness: "As a member of the white
women's movement, I have not confronted the terror of difference.

I have sought to obliterate it in connections."[23] She goes on to affirm many of the skills white women have learned in making relational and social connections, yet she ultimately leaves us indicted when she says, "This learning has its strengths, but in relation to cultural and racial difference, it should be defined as sin for white women."[24] Here is yet another feminist writer who has so particularized the praxis of sin that it has the possibility of informing and transforming the specific social and ethical behavior of white women.

Deconstructing and reconstructing our understandings of sin and evil are not just the tasks of feminist and womanist theologians, but the tasks of all of us in a day when crucifixions abound. In an effort to challenge preachers to look critically at the ways so many of us seem to understand and speak about the nature and patterns of sin, David Buttrick, in his *The Mystery and the Passion*, asks this question:

> What crucified Christ? Why, our inner fears and guilts, hostilities and anxieties; the cross happened because of a human pathology. Nowadays, sin is primarily a psychological problem; it is a "heart disease." Whether sin is labeled hubris or egocentricity or overreaching desire, it is located within the self, in individual selves, and is expressed in a range of unsavory symptoms, especially anxiety and hostility. . . . For nearly fifty years, preachers have described sin as an inner fault that seems to show up primarily in a pattern of psychological symptoms.[25]

Then, after exposing the limitations of contemporary preaching in its reduction of sin to the action of an isolated, individual self, Buttrick reminds us of the truth that lies at the heart of Jesus' crucifixion and all human crucifixions:

> Remember, crucifixion was a Roman punishment for political crime. . . . Who crucified Christ? Not human being as a psychological isolate—the self, in fears and guilts and hates. No. Christ was crucified by human beings in their social patterns.[26]

We can quickly see the implications of our proclamations about sin and evil. If sin is that which is done by the individual self, then engaging in individualized repentance and seeking personal forgiveness become the needed actions. If sin and evil are understood as having political, social, systemic roots and realities, then individual and collective conversion and organized resistance become the called for and necessary actions. It is never that individual repentance is unimportant; it simply is not enough to stop the social and political crucifixions that strip people of their humanity and their lives.

In our preaching ministries, do we continue to make universal, uncontexualized pronouncements about the nature and practice of sin or do we particularize and contextualize our theological understandings of sin and evil? Do we continue to emphasize individualistic, privatized understandings of sin and evil over social, systemic expressions of sin and evil? Does our preaching ministry enable the particular communities in which we reside to name and own the particular expressions of sin and evil that distinctly relate to the privileges of ethnicity, class, gender, age, sexual orientation, able-bodied mobility, and health? Enabling individuals and whole communities to understand sin and evil in new and deepened ways is critical in a preaching ministry that will also enable those same communities to name the oppression and crucifixions that those expressions of sin and evil produce.

> The sixth and final task for a preaching ministry that seeks to resist crucifixions centers around preachers analyzing and critiquing a cluster of theological issues directly connected to the cross and Jesus' death by crucifixion.

Latin American liberation theologians continue to be some of the voices that have helped me understand more clearly how sacrificial theologies that affirm suffering, crosses, and self-sacrifice serve to undergird and condone incessant violence and modern-day crucifixions. Their theologies of the cross, understandings of redemption and salvation, and affirmations of resurrection are essentially different from the dominant white European and dominant white North American theology still espoused in most of our churches. Their work, along with that of white Euro-American and Canadian feminists, Asian feminists, African feminists, African American womanists, *mujerista* women, gay and lesbian theologians, and theologians from within the disabilities community, has convinced me we must move toward theologies of the cross that work in the service of liberation.

When Christian preachers face the reality of Jesus' crucifixion on the cross, many theological questions and issues must be addressed, two of which I want to explore here: How do we explain why it happened? What do the cross and Jesus' crucifixion say about the nature of God and God's activity in the world? Let us take a brief look at how many Christian preachers have answered these questions.

How Do We Explain Why It Happened?

One of the answers to this question has produced a certain cluster of theological justifications that have dominated Christian preaching throughout the centuries. The language may vary, but the theological substance remains very similar. We need to remember that these perspectives are historical, theological constructions which have been shaped by Christian people throughout the centuries in a faithful attempt to respond to the most crucial questions that arise around Jesus' crucifixion. And just as they evolved over time, new theological understandings are rising up to challenge and reshape those traditional responses.

One of the primary interpretations of Jesus' crucifixion on the cross suggests that it happened as an act of atonement. In order for human beings to be reconciled to God, instead of remaining in a permanent state of alienation, God preplanned, premeditated, and fully intended the death of Jesus as a sacrifice that would adequately and fully compensate for the sinfulness of humanity. In the satisfaction theory of atonement, human sin is offensive to God's sense of justice, and, thus, Jesus' sacrifice is a satisfactory form of reparation to please God. In the ransom theory of atonement, human beings are overpowered by Satan and the powers of evil, and Jesus is the ransom offered to redeem and free us. In atonement as expiation, human sin must be punished and Jesus becomes our atoning sacrifice. Even though human beings deserve to be punished and to die, he suffers and dies in our place. What is at stake in all of these atonement theories is a punitive God and a sacrificial offering.

In 1988, Rita Nakashima Brock, in *Journeys by Heart: A Christology of Erotic Power*, forged one of the most startling and radical critiques that has been waged against atonement christologies. Even though many voices have been drawing upon her work for over a decade now, her words were the ones that courageously expanded the serious feminist critique of atonement theology that was in the process of being constructed:

> Atonement christologies contain some notion of original sin, in which humanity is believed to be born with a tragic flaw. . . . The punishment of one perfect child has to occur before the father can forgive the rest of his children and love them. . . . The sacrifice of this perfect son is the way to new life with the father for all those, who in their freedom, choose to believe someone else's suffering can atone for our flawed nature. The death and resurrection of this child are celebrated as salvific.[27]

We live in a day in which family violence is at an all-time high. In this country, one in every three daughters and one in every seven sons are molested by the age of eighteen. Every six minutes, a woman is raped in the United States. Battering is a major cause of injury to adult women, and marital rape is a very common kind of sexual assault.[28] Atonement christologies that focus on divine sacrifice in any way become a part of the theological justification for such violence. If Jesus' suffering on a cross is seen and proclaimed as virtuous and righteous, then human beings who suffer on crosses must be virtuous and righteous as well.

As a profound alternative to such atonement christologies, Brock suggests that redemptive activity and work take place within what she calls, "Christa/community."[29] It is within community that suffering is healed and oppression is resisted. No one person can save human persons from the sinfulness of social evil; rather, all faithful persons are called to participate in the mending and healing of creation. Brock says, "The shift in perspective suggested here relocates Christ in the community of which Jesus is one historical part."[30] The power that is at the heart of this community is erotic power, the power of love, the power of heart.[31] And redemption happens in all times and in all places where communities of people decide to live this erotic power and love with abandonment and conviction.

Brock not only critiques traditional atonement theology, she offers us a christology of community. No longer can the incarnation of God as the Christ be reduced to Jesus or any one individual person. Rather, the incarnational, redemptive power of God now resides within the community. It is in that same community, and countless human communities, that believers work for the mending of our relationship with God and all creation offering a profound alternative to a punitive God and a sacrificial offering.

Closely related to the notion of Jesus as sacrificial lamb is Jesus as suffering servant, Jesus as the one who battles Satan in order to reclaim fallen humanity. This theology suggests Jesus is the New Covenant, the one who is victorious over sin. In all these interpretations, Jesus is destined to endure suffering and agony in order to transform the power of sin and to establish a new relationship, a new promise or covenant, between God and humanity.

Jon Sobrino summarizes these theological explanations in these words: "Jesus is innocent, the sufferings he bears are those that others ought to bear and by bearing them he becomes salvation for others."[32]

Human beings are not held accountable, rather Jesus as the suffering servant intervenes to re-establish a new relationship between God and humanity.

All of these traditional theological explanations and justifications for why Jesus was crucified on the cross are just that: They are *justifications*. They rationalize, spiritualize, romanticize and raise to religious saintly status the concrete reality of suffering and the specific reality of Jesus' murderous crucifixion. Also, they are explanations that are far removed from the concrete, material, and historical realities of Jesus' time. They are explanations that suggest that Jesus did not in fact experience the same kind of death that other human beings do. Thus, his particular crucifixion was infinitely removed from the political and social crucifixions that have happened through the centuries.

As a profound alternative, the well-known Chinese theologian C. S. Song urges us to clearly and uncompromisingly view and interpret the cross as human violence.[33] He urges us to see that traditional ways of interpreting the cross have spoken about evil powers as mostly outside the realities of suffering and death that actual human beings experience at the hands of one another:[34]

> The cross means human beings rejecting human beings. It is human beings abandoning human beings. . . . And the cross discloses the complicity of socio-political powers ready to defend their self-interest at any cost. . . It was not planned by his Abba-God, but by human beings.[35]

If Rita Nakashima Brock's critique of atonement theology reveals to us a distortion of God and shows us how God has become a divine child abuser in the traditional theology of the Christian church, C. S. Song's critique of atonement theology reveals to us a distortion of human beings and shows us a painfully clear picture of what human beings are willing to do to one another in the name of religion and within the unchecked bounds of political and social power. Their words call out to preachers to reshape our theology around the cross so that we might deconstruct the distortions of both God and humanity in order to hold humanity more accountable for the unspeakable violence we are capable of doing to one another. These are radical words that call into question many of the traditional teachings and theology of the Christian church.

A thorough and profound critique is being waged against sacrificial, atonement christologies by people who are oppressed and who have experienced firsthand the painful, oppressive ramifications of this theology. Preachers who are committed to resisting contemporary forms of injustice and crucifixion must wrestle with these indicting prophets and reformers and hopefully join their voices to those who would give radically new and different answers to the question, *Why was Jesus crucified?*

What Do the Cross and Jesus' Crucifixion Say about the Nature of God and God's Activity in the World?

The first question about "why" Jesus was crucified raised issues of explanation as well as questions about the activity of God. With this question, I want to move a little further and more directly into a few specific questions about God's identity and nature. We cannot face the cross and Jesus' crucifixion without asking questions about the nature of God and God's activity. Both Brock and Song have already confronted us with this truth. Is God a vengeful, punitive God who demands some kind of appeasement or sacrifice in order to forgive and love humanity? Is God a sadist? A divine child abuser? Is God a God of love and justice, who with limited power due to human freedom can only weep in the face of Jesus' death on a cross? Is God a God of suffering, who not only weeps, but actually suffers with Jesus on the cross? Is God silent and uninvolved? Is God a distanced observer?

Even though I continue to believe that these questions will not lead us to the same kind of human agency and response as the previous questions (Where are human beings? What does the cross say about human sinfulness and violence?), they are still questions that are at the heart of my own faith questioning and perhaps at the heart of most of Christendom.

During the entire process of writing my second book on systemic evil and the preacher's response to it, I was absolutely focused on the question of human agency. Now as I seek to move toward a theology and homiletic of resurrection, it has been powerful to find that I am returning to these questions about God and God's activity in the world with full force.

Even though I know that in interpreting God and the cross, countless Christian preachers have embraced an understanding of God that is punitive, a God that demands retribution, a God that sacrifices God's own son—these are all affirmations I want to thoroughly denounce. I cannot believe in a God whose nature and activity give rise to such violent implications and realities.

In this section on the nature of God and God's activity in relation to the cross, I want to reflect on two distinct theological interpretations. The first is the image of a suffering/crucified God. The second is the image of a silent God. In looking at the image of a suffering God, I will focus on Latin American theologians in particular. To focus on an understanding of a silent God, I will focus exclusively on the work of C. S. Song.

Suffering/Crucified God

Latin American liberation theologians have been offering us a variety of theological understandings of a suffering/crucified God for well over two decades.[36] For these theologians, God not only suffers with Jesus on the cross, but actually is crucified with him. God's nature is one of compassion and solidarity, choosing to be fully present to Jesus and with Jesus. Yet, understanding God as a crucified God also suggests more than God's presence. It suggests that in Jesus' crucifixion God's own being is there on the cross as well. However, the nature of God's compassion and mercy and the suffering activity of God are not limited only to Jesus. For many Latin American theologians, affirming that God both suffers and is crucified on the cross with Jesus is a prelude to affirming that God suffers with all people who suffer and God is crucified with the crucified people of history. Wherever people are violated, God is violated; wherever people are tortured, God is tortured; wherever people are crucified, God is crucified.

As profound as these affirmations are, they still leave essential questions unanswered. Does this mean that God is utterly immanent and has no ability to transcend the human arena and condition? Does this mean that God, still all-powerful and all-present, chooses to suffer and chooses to join humanity on the crosses they bear out of divine love and compassion? What does this say about the reality of the incarnation, God with us, and revealed in us? Does God suffer and experience crucifixion because God is revealed and present in each one of us and in all creation? Even once you have affirmed that God suffers with Jesus and with us, or that God was crucified on the same cross that crucified Jesus and on all subsequent crosses, there is much more to be understood and said about the nature and activity of God.

There is also a serious critique to wage against this theological interpretation as well as some critical questions with which preachers must struggle. As preachers, we need to understand that to affirm that God is crucified with the crucified of history is to say something very important about God's nature and activity; yet it is to once again remain painfully silent about what must be done to stop those crucifixions. It is comforting to believe that God never abandons us, is present with us in every conceivable form of suffering and violence, *and* that comforting belief and affirmation alone will not alleviate or stop unjust violence and crucifixion.

Patricia Wismer says, "The suffering God does indeed provide comfort, companionship, and perhaps hope to us in our afflictions, as well as actualizing in some credible way the meaning of God's goodness and love."[37] But in citing the critique that many feminist theologians and women of faith are raising, she asks, "Exactly how, they ask, does God's suffering with us actually help eliminate, or at least mitigate, our suffering?"[38]

In many ways this critique alone would be enough to give any preacher pause in believing that suffering/crucified God language is enough to address how God responds to human crucifixions of every kind. Even though I can appreciate much about these affirmations, I question whether they will lead to concrete human action.

The inadequacy of these affirmations is one critique, yet perhaps there is an even more serious one to consider as we think about preaching this theology. Regardless of what our theological positions are regarding the relationship of Jesus and God, it is not difficult to see that affirming a suffering/crucified God is akin to affirming a suffering/crucified Jesus, and then to see that we are still giving credence and power to the same traditional notions of enduring and affirming suffering. Returning to Rebecca Parker and Joanne Brown's work, even after they affirm that they believe that the theology of a suffering God is theological advancement in comparison to a sadist God of retribution, they still share an important critique:

> Because God suffers and God is good, we are good if we suffer. If we are not suffering, we are not good. To be like God is to take on the pain of all. In this form of piety, pain becomes attractive—the more we suffer the more we can believe we approach God. . . . This theology is offensive because it suggests that acceptance of pain is tantamount to love and is the foundation of social action.[39]

A God of suffering compassion is a profound alternative to a distant, detached God who does not directly experience any of the suffering and agony Jesus experiences on the cross. This understanding is an alternative to a God who directly chooses the cross for Jesus' life and thereby inflicts the suffering of the crucifixion. Does this theological perspective, when preached, continue to add its voice and support for righteous suffering and perpetuate the belief that suffering is at the heart of the Christian faith, not life?

The Silent God

C. S. Song offers in his book, *Jesus, the Crucified People,* a thorough critique of the God of retribution[40] and suggests that the cross is a scandal to human beings and a scandal to God.[41] Then he turns to the questions of God's nature and God's activity in response to the cross that crucified Jesus and to all crosses that crucify humanity. In what Song labels as his "biography of God"[42] (which is what any and all human beings create as we attempt to give expression to who God is and what God does in the world), he seeks to wrestle with how God responds to the cross that crucified Jesus. In doing so, Song looks at God through the lens of several images, all of which will lead him eventually to a God of silence.

First, he looks at God as "The Speaking God."[43] He reminds us that in most biographies that have been created and written about God, God is primarily portrayed as a speaking God. God speaks in scripture, God speaks in human history, God speaks in our lives. "The God who created heaven and earth and all things is a speaking God,"[44] and as powerful as words are, Song believes they are not always adequate vehicles for God and for human beings. Human beings honor each other with speech; we also betray and violate each other. There are angry words, deceiving words, slanderous words, and punitive, judging words. Words are often inadequate in the face of human pain and suffering, and words can destroy.[45] Ultimately words are not enough, even God's words.

Second, he looks at "The Listening God."[46] The same God who speaks also listens to humanity and creation. Song draws particularly upon the prophets who lay before us countless images of God listening, God taking heed, God bending God's heart and mind and soul toward creation. If God were not a listening God, our prayers would be without hope, without meaning. "God is willing to listen,"[47] and this simple affirmation says volumes about the nature of God and God's activity in relation to all creation.

The third image of God which Song explores is "The Remembering God."[48] God remembers humanity tenderly and never forgets us. God keeps track of us. God holds us in God's eternal memory. God not only remembers humanity, but yearns/longs to be intimately connected to us and to all creation. "God's memory is the hope of humanity. It is the hope of all creation."[49] This remembering God is a God who vows to not disregard, forget, or forsake us—not in the past, not now, not ever.

The Silent God is the fourth image of God that Song turns to in an effort to understand the fullness of God's nature and activity.[50] In the face of such a horrible thing as the crucifixion of Jesus, has God become silent? In a powerful way Song says, "But the God who has been speaking incessantly since the beginning of creation has, all of a sudden, stopped speaking."[51]

This is in contrast to what we have come to believe about Jesus and God. Jesus has counted on God's voice and God's speaking throughout his life and ministry, but when he most needs God to speak, has God become utterly silent? "The speaking God expected the speaking Jesus. The speaking Jesus needed the speaking God."[52]—Song believes that this silence is exactly what has prompted the kind of atonement theologies the church has created—some powerful way to explain the silence, to actually take the silence away, to remedy what appears to be so great a contradiction in God's own nature and activity that it cannot be tolerated by human beings, thus, we create endless justifications and explanations.

Song does not embrace traditional explanations of God's silence, nor does he feel the need to justify Jesus' crucifixion with any kind of atonement or sacrificial theology. Yet, he continues to wrestle with the silence and what it means. He believes Jesus' death was so horrible it shocked God into silence.[53]

Song confronts us with a grieving God who is quiet in the face of the devastation of profound grief. Perhaps the silence of God is "a silence of protest."[54] God's silence echoes and resounds through the universe as God grieves and protests the injustice, and the violence, done to Jesus and to creation. "What disgrace you have done to your own humanity!" That scandal is too much even for God.[55]

The final image of God that flows from the God of silence is the *Karuna* of God.[56] *Karuna* means two important things for Song's theology. First, *karuna* means a kind of pity and compassion that does not just extend to an exclusive few but is the kind of compassion that exists for and extends to all. The second meaning of *karuna* is "the womb treasury" or the source of life from which all things are produced and created. Song says, "Pity (*karuna*) is like a womb in which life is created, nourished, and empowered."[57]

Song believes that the womb of God is that which is surrounding

Jesus in his final moments of death, and that womb is compassion, pity. And just as life is nourished in a womb in that silence which is a profound part of the life that grows, develops, and is transformed there, so does the womb of God provide the environment, the assurance, the silent fullness that will eventually enable Jesus' transformation:

> That silence of God is like a womb enveloping Jesus on the cross, empowering him during the last moments of his life and nourishing him for the resurrection of a new life from the tomb.... No language is necessary, for that womb of God is God's language.[58]

This womb of God's own being, this womb of God's own silence, this womb of God's own life-giving power will hold Jesus until he has become the resurrected one.

There are some serious questions to raise in response to the image of a silent God, even when that silence is seen as a womb of life. The first critique is similar to one I waged in response to the image of a suffering God. Just as the image of a suffering God might serve to ultimately sanction human suffering as godlike and holy, could not the image of a silent God also serve to perpetuate and sanction silence as holy, sacred response to the crucifixions of our day? Though silence can be filled with protest and resistance in very distinct, dramatic ways, it often is filled with denial and passivity. Whereas the suffering-God images offer a source of reassurance about the active presence of God along with the one who suffers, does the silent God offer such comfort and reassurance? Once again, it is true that silence can be full, poignant, sensitive, and filled with compassion. It is equally true that silence emerges from the gulf of social distance, the alienation of privileged lives, and a profound sense of self protection. In the actual moments of absolute quiet, how is the one who is suffering to comprehend and experience the silence? In a time when women and men have struggled to claim the image of "breaking silence" as the first step of redemptive activity in stopping violence against women and violence against children, will the image of a silent God be used to justify and sustain a multitude of violences shrouded in silence?

Another serious challenge related to the image of the silent God, which ultimately in Song's theology becomes the nourishing womb of God, is how to relate that image to the redemptive activity of human beings. The suffering God challenges human beings to so embrace and enter into another's suffering that one suffers simultaneously. This kind of compassion and solidarity can be seen and heard in the daily struggles, decisions, and actions of all kinds of human beings. The silent God, the womb of God, extending God's own self in such a way as to surround Jesus, is a more difficult image to translate into concrete human action. How do human beings surround one another with a nourishing womb so that resurrected life can emerge on the other side of crucifixion? And when human beings are actually able to surround each other with such nourishing life as to enable resurrection, how might we describe those moments as highly active and engaged even though, as wombs are hidden from our sight, these activities may not be as visible? Perhaps Song needs to carry his *karuna*/womb-of-God image even further and help us know what this redemptive activity looks like when human beings struggle against crucifixions.

Another aspect of Song's silent womb of God is the waiting and the implication that resurrection life cannot be experienced until life in the womb has come to fruition. We know this affirmation of life to be true for life growing in a woman's womb. It cannot be rushed; it must be waited upon with patience and hope. We can even imagine the womb of God ultimately giving birth to a resurrected Jesus. When we focus on God and God's activity, these images seem powerful, mysterious, and true to much of what we know about life, resurrection, transformation. But when we consider these images from the perspective of those who are dying in this very moment or who are suffering unbearable agony, violence, and torture, the waiting required in the womb of God seems far less comforting.

Song says, "The silence will be broken when the womb completes its task, when the womb ejects that life out into the world."[59] In terms of our understanding of human pregnancy, we know this to be utterly true. Also, we know that sometimes the pregnancy, sometimes the waiting, can seem like an eternity, can seem almost unbearable. Could not the waiting that is necessary even in the silent womb of God ultimately become one more justification for endurance and patient suffering?

Alternatives to the Suffering God and the Silent Womb of God

In contrast to an utterly distanced God, a God of retribution, a sadist God, or a divine child abuser, the theological constructions of suffering God theology and silent womb of God theology are redemptive steps forward. As this section concludes, let us turn to two alternative images that no preacher can ignore in response to the questions about God and God's activity in response to the cross.

An Angry God. A number of years ago a friend of mine returned from a trip to the Philippines. She brought me two gifts: a beautiful handmade necklace and a photograph she had taken of a painting that was entitled "The Angry Christ."[60] I have cherished that photo for many years, even though the rage in the eyes of the Christ figure is haunting and somewhat terrifying. However, as haunting as it is, the depiction of the Christ is also enormously liberating and empowering as I have thought of injustice and crucifixion. When I look at it, I see righteous indignation, lament, clarity of rage. There is a finger being pointed directly out at the onlooker. It is the finger of indictment, the finger of accountability. I want to hold onto this depiction and to lift it up for our serious consideration in terms of God's nature and activity. If we are ever to resist fully the unjust crucifixions that abound, not only do human beings need to reclaim the language and action of lament, we need to claim a God who cries out in redemptive anger and holy outrage. We need a God who comforts and is present with those who are suffering. We need a God who is angry about that suffering and who is willing to hold people accountable.

Song shares a Korean parable about the powerful witness of anger and resistance and how it fuels a whole people's resistance. He tells the story of a poor man who was tortured and mutilated by the powerful and wealthy. All he had left was his torso, but day and night he would roll from wall to wall creating a sound that filled the city streets and could not be silenced. The final lines of the parable read:

ᐁᐁ

> Some people say it is the work of a ghost,
> Others that it is An-do who did not die but is still alive, somewhere,
> rolling his trunk from wall to wall . . .
> The latter, as they whisper this story in the streets of Seoul, have a
> strange fire in their eyes.[61]

Maybe God is a God who has fiery eyes and who is not only known to us in silence and suffering but in relentless, grueling anger and resistance.

My whole life I have been told stories about the fear of those who witnessed Jesus' crucifixion. The disciples entered into acts of betrayal and fled. The women, at least present, watched from a distance. What I have never been encouraged to believe or consider is the possible rage, anger, and outrage that might have simultaneously existed in those early followers. These are human emotions as normal and natural as fear and betrayal. Perhaps until we can imagine an angry, indignant God, it will remain almost impossible for us to consider angry disciples.

But I believe they must have been haunted, and they must have been outraged, for betrayal and fear alone could not have raised an early church, could not have fueled a resurrection community.

Song returns to the image of fire, and, even though he does not use the image to suggest that God is angry or that the early Christian community was angry, I still hear his words calling us to a God who resists, not just a God who suffers:

> And it could have been that strange fire in the eyes of those women who watched Jesus' crucifixion that made them the first witnesses of his resurrection. Even his disciples, who deserted him, must have had that strange fire in their eyes when they began to tell the story of the life and death of their master later. It must have been that strange fire in the eyes that inspired them to become bold witnesses to his message of God's reign.[62]

An angry God, outraged and lamenting and calling for accountability, empowers a people who are able to be and do the same. It is not the anger of destruction and punishment but the anger of life and resistance.

The God Who Takes People from the Cross. One of Jon Sobrino's latest books is entitled *The Principle of Mercy: Taking the Crucified People from the Cross.*[63] The volume focuses on the central mission of the church—that of showing mercy and removing people from the crosses that crucify them. A God whose nature is mercy is akin to the God who suffers on the cross with the crucified of history, and even akin to the God who wraps a nourishing womb of silence around Jesus on the cross. However, the activities of mercy in Sobrino's understanding all have to do with concrete acts that take crucified people down from the crosses that violate and kill them. This God and this activity stand in stark contrast to a God who suffers on the cross with the crucified, a God whose womb will bring about resurrection on the other side of crucifixion. Borrowing the image from Sobrino (who borrows it from Ignácio Ellacuria), we now face a God whose activity is removing people from the cross. This powerful alternative image is capable of informing and empowering the resistance activity of God's people. Now God is not only wherever people suffer and are waiting for resurrection and transformation, but everywhere and in every action where people are taken down from every conceivable cross that crucifies them. Just because human beings are not miraculously saved from specific crucifixions does not mean God is not acting.

Maybe when Jesus was hanging on the cross, God was raising up a community that would resist crosses and become committed to taking people from them for all eternity. God was not waiting to act until Jesus was dead. God was acting throughout Jesus' ministry in ways that would ultimately raise up a community of people who would refuse to abandon life. God was raising up that resistance community in the very moments of Jesus' death. This did not remove Jesus from the concrete suffering of his cross, but God's mercy and protest were shaping a radical religious community that would resist crosses and crucifixions for centuries to come. As preachers seeking to resist crucifixions in every way possible, we join our lives to that radical mission of the early Christian church. God does not just suffer with the crucified of history, nor is God reduced to only silence. God actively raised up a resurrection community in Jesus' lifetime, and God is able to do the same in our generation. For now, may all of us who would engage in preaching ministries seeking to resist the crucifixions that destroy people be haunted and challenged by Ignácio Ellacuria's words once more: "Ask yourselves: what have I done to crucify them? What do I do to uncrucify them? What must I do for this people to rise again?"[64]

ANGUISH—A RIVER OF POSSIBILITY

Read Mark 11: 15–19 and Joel 2:1–2, 12–17a

A number of years ago, when I was teaching at Princeton Seminary, a man in one of my classes preached a very moving sermon dealing with human suffering. A friend of his was dying from AIDS. When the sermon was finished, Nick sat down, and, in typical fashion, the class and I began to discuss the sermon. We were all struggling to understand the pain of what he had just described and somehow to make some sense of it.

Most of our conversation centered around a scene Nick had shared from Elie Wiesel's story, "Night." In that story about the Holocaust which many of us know well, Wiesel recalls a day when two adults and one child were about to be hung, and a person behind him says, "Where is God?" And then as they are forced to walk past the gallows within full sight of the small child's body still struggling for life, the question comes again, "Where is God now?" And a small voice within Wiesel answers, "Where is God? God is here—God is hanging here on this gallows."[65]

At some point in the process, I came into the conversation in a more impassioned way. I shared that this profound story had helped me make sense of human suffering and injustice. Over the years, that question and the belief that God is present in our suffering have brought me some peace, some strange comfort.

I quietly ended my testimony, and then a very reflective, thoughtful student said, "So what, Chris. So what? The boy still died." And then she began to cry. And as she did, her question, "So what?" made all of us push past easy answers and platitudes, even the strangely comforting answer that God is hanging on the gallows.

Not long after that moment, I was reading a book where the a question, "Why is it we ask where is God?" Why don't we ask, "Where are human beings?" I knew in an instant why this woman's "So what?" was so utterly confrontive. Children still hang from gallows, even when God is present. God is there when millions of human beings starve yearly and the homeless freeze to death. God is there as refugees walk dusty roads back to devastated homelands and indigenous people lose more and more sacred land each year. God is there when women are battered and raped by people they love and people with disabilities are shut into institutions and out of public life. God is there hanging on the gallows, weeping tears of despair, crying out in pain; and crosses that inflict pain upon our sisters and brothers still abound with unmerciful persistence.

It is no happenstance that this woman preacher, the one who had the courage to say, "So what? The child still died," is an incest survivor. She is angry. She is hurt. She has been robbed and exploited. Each time we find any kind of easy comfort in a God who hangs on the gallows instead of finding courage to rage and grieve against the gallows, she is shouting to us, "So what? I still died."

From the heart of anguish, she confronts the comfortable and distanced—so many of us—with an unbearable truth. Each time she confronts us with her anguish, it might feel like only a few tables overturned and a few coins scattered. Will it be enough to bring the seat of power down and transform the lives of those abused?

Perhaps it is too easy for those of us who have not experienced the degradation and horror of inflicted suffering and injustice to say that it is enough that God is present. How about *our* presence? It is too easy to proclaim God's tender constancy while a girl child is molested by her mother or raped by her father. How about *our* tender constancy? It is even too easy to affirm that God weeps when a bashed gay man weeps and mourns, when a mother cannot feed her children. But how about *our* weeping and *our* mourning?

During these experiences of suffering, the cries of humanity and creation are begging us to scatter the proud, to bring down the powerful, to send the rich away empty, and to lift up the lowly. In the immediate moments of human pain, children, men, women cry out for it to stop and for God and humanity together to do something.

"Then they came to Jerusalem. And he entered the temple and began to drive out those who were selling and those who were buying in the temple, and he overturned the tables of the money changers and the seats of those who sold doves; and he would not allow anyone to carry anything through the temple."

It is difficult for our contemporary minds to fathom both the real and symbolic power of the Temple at this point in Jesus' ministry. Immense buildings occupying acres and acres of land, the Temple is the center of religious and economic life. All the buyers and sellers, all the commercial activity would not have surprised or shocked Jesus. This was common Temple life. But the unjust social realities underneath all this activity shocked and angered him until the day he died.

It has never been difficult for me to imagine Jesus angry, indignant, outraged. His confrontation with the money changers and the merchants seems utterly consistent with all that he stood for in his ministry and life. I would expect Jesus to be outraged by a system that required exploitive taxes from the poor and sacrificial doves from women and those who had leprosy. Those who were considered ritually unclean were required to make sacrifices as a penance for their inferior status. I would expect him to be outraged. However, what has captured my heart and spirit has been trying to imagine what Jesus must have felt underneath the anger, underneath the outrage, for perhaps no other single moment in his ministry sealed his death quite like this one. What would have been important enough, even horrible enough, to compel him to directly confront the entire Temple and all it stood for? It might be like one solitary human being trying to shut down the Pentagon, or stop the creation of nuclear warheads, or influence a multinational corporation.

Julia Esquivel, an exiled Guatemalan poet, helps me move closer to what Jesus must have been feeling with her words in the following poem.

The Sigh ⌒⌒

When it is necessary to drink so much pain,
when a river of anguish
drowns us,
when we have wept many tears
and they flow like rivers
from our sad eyes,
only then
does the deep hidden sigh of our neighbor
become our own.[66]

Jesus has been drinking so much pain, has wept so many tears, has been close to so many who hurt. He is swimming in a river of anguish. He has felt so many hidden sighs of so many neighbors, and they have all become his own. When he walks into the Temple that day, he sees children with outstretched arms. He sees the head of John the Baptist. He sees a widow with a few coins. He sees a woman who has been bleeding and isolated for twelve years. He sees hungry crowds, repentant tax collectors. He sees a strong Canaanite woman and a grieving rich young ruler. Their faces, their lives compel him as only a river of anguish can. What is at stake here for Jesus is everything. He is a Jewish rabbi anguished by the practices of his own people. He is not outraged at a few isolated, exploiting merchants, nor is he most concerned with the spiritual nature of God's house. He is anguished over an entire system that oppresses the masses while the social and religious elite prosper. He has a mighty vision of grace and justice and a call from God that will not let him rest. And everywhere he looks, the world reveals such a stark, painful contrast.

He has come to a moment when weeping is not enough. He places his body in direct resistance to the powers that exploit. Those with social and religious power keep looking for a way to kill him, and the crowd is spellbound.

Will a few overturned tables and scattered coins bring the seat of power down and transform the lives of the poor? Maybe . . .

Jesus' life and ministry have given rise to liberation movements that have given people back their humanity. His spirit and his resurrection power have been a force for radical change where people have lost all hope.

There are times that members of the human family reach their own temple moments, moments when they cannot remain silent any longer. They cannot live with the death, the bloodshed, the violence any more. It is like anguish bursting forth like a gushing well. It cannot be contained or ignored or silenced or denied one moment longer.

From 1976 to 1990, the school children of South Africa adopted a campaign of resistance against apartheid. Seven hundred and fifty children were killed; many more were assaulted and tortured. There is a moment in the movie *Sarafina!* where we glimpse a vision of the children's anguish as we imagine thousands of children with torches held high walking through the streets of Soweto singing:

> You can wound us
> But you can't stop us . . .
> We are coming.
>
> ∞
>
> You can kill us
> But we will live again . . .
> We are coming.
>
> ∞
>
> Sharpen your spears
> The war is at your door . . .
> We are coming.[67]

The children of South Africa had reached a moment where weeping was not enough. They had drunk so much pain, and they had already wept a river of tears. Their anguish forced them to place their bodies in direct resistance to the powers of injustice. And when they did, the whole nation, the entire globe, was spellbound. With absolute clarity one imprisoned child said: "They hurt us to make us fear them. We fear them, but we do not forget. We are still children, we are young and full of fear, but every day we grow older, we grow stronger, we do not forget."

Could any of us forget? Could we forget that our fathers have been taken from our homes and killed? Could we forget that we were never allowed to study our own history? Could we forget whips on our back or dogs biting at our legs? Could we forget our homes burned down or our mothers spending their whole lives taking care of white children in the city? These realities would fill any human heart and spirit with enough rage and anguish that children, young and full of fear, would take to the streets against an entire government.

At the time, even eight thousand children imprisoned must have felt like a few tables overturned and a handful of scattered coins. Would it bring down the seat of power and transform the lives of the poor? Maybe, just maybe.

June 17, 1991 —Apartheid laws appealed

May 10, 1994 —Nelson Mandela elected first black president of South Africa.

"Is it not written, my house shall be called a house of prayer for all the nations? But you have made it a den of robbers."

Jesus is anguished that the Temple has become something so far from a house for all the nations, so far from a house of welcome for all God's people, and so far from a place of God's limitless hospitality that he likens it to a den where robbers divide their spoil. Jesus is speaking directly from the prophets Isaiah and Jeremiah: Isaiah, who heralded the day when all the dispossessed of the world would be welcomed in the Temple; and Jeremiah, who would never allow the people to forget that if the Temple became a place of exploitation and exclusion, it would come crashing down to rubble.

This Temple scene is as real today as it was in that moment long ago. There are crowds of oppressed people and there are the privileged elite. There is unspeakable injustice everywhere we look, *and* there are contemporary prophets overturning their own tables and scattering what coins they can.

❖   Gay men and lesbians are saying: Is it not written, God's house shall be called a house of grace? But you have made it a den of condemnation.

❖   People with disabilities are saying: Is it not written, God's house shall be called a house of gracious hospitality? But you have made it a place of insurmountable barriers.

❖   Children who are physically and sexually abused are saying: Is it not written, God's house shall be called a house of safety? But you have made it a place where abusers can hide easily.

❖   Older adults who are alone and marginalized are saying: Is it not written, God's house shall be called a house of holy respect? But you have made it a place where we bow to the idol of youthfulness.

❖   The working poor are saying: Is it not written, God's house shall be called a house of justice? But you have made it a place of shameful blaming.

I sometimes fear that we have become robbers in the house of God. Is not the rubble beginning to tumble down around us?

Perhaps we never know the full weight or impact of what expressed anguish can do in the world, where it leads, the difference it makes, what changes it helps bring about, what systems it brings down, what liberation it births, what misery it might stop.

"Yet even now," says our God, "return to me with all your heart, with fasting, with weeping, and with mourning; and rend your hearts and not your garments."

This is the kind of repentance that just might save us if we tear our hearts and break them open, if we find it necessary to drink so much pain. If we feel every hidden sigh of our neighbor and let ourselves be immersed in a river of anguish, there will be many tables to overturn and a multitude of coins to scatter.

4

Risking the Terror of Resurrection

In this chapter we turn explicitly to the resurrection as it is portrayed in the gospel narratives, with only slight references to the Pauline letters. I turn to the scriptures in an effort to lift up some of what I consider to be the radical gospel embedded there and to articulate some of the claims that radical gospel might make on our preaching ministries. The sermon following this chapter is based on the John 20:19–31 passage that appears in the common lectionary on the second Sunday of Easter in all three cycles.

Knowing that there are many skilled biblical scholars who are able to provide the Christian preacher with detailed exegetical information about these texts, I will not attempt a thorough exegetical analysis of these resurrection narratives. Rather, I will make some homiletical observations about the challenges these narratives pose to all of us who would preach about the resurrection of Jesus in particular and about God's resurrection power and possibility in general.

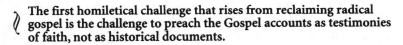

The first homiletical challenge that rises from reclaiming radical gospel is the challenge to preach the Gospel accounts as testimonies of faith, not as historical documents.

Differences in the Gospel Traditions

It has become clear to most preachers today that the Gospel accounts of the resurrection of Jesus are just that: narrative accounts, portrayals, testimonies. They were never intended to be historical accounts. "They are," as the biblical scholar Robert Smith notes, "Easter books from beginning to end, penned by people who in various ways—not in the same way—knew Jesus as raised from the dead, forever alive, and mighty."[1] Smith is certainly one of those scholars who firmly believes the Gospels were all written from a post-resurrection perspective that deeply influenced all of the Gospels, even though each one of them bears witness to that resurrection in a distinct way. He goes on to say,

From their first pages to their last the evangelists have supplied the passports and papers of identification, not of one who once walked the earth only to disappear in dust and ashes, but of the one who today continues to meet the congregation and to confront the world.[2]

The Gospels were accounts that were carefully crafted with certain communities of faith in mind. They were shaped for particular social and religious contexts and were textured by the social location and faith of each particular author. They reflect the passion, the faith, and the theology of those authors and the great sense of accountability they felt toward the religious communities of which they were a part. It should not surprise us, then, that there are great differences between the resurrection accounts recorded in Mark, Matthew, Luke, and John—differences that give us a very complex, multidimensional view and understanding of the resurrection of Jesus and the early church's interpretation of it. Let me name just a few of those differences:

Place: Mark and Matthew identify the place of Jesus' appearances as Galilee while Luke and John identify the place of the appearances as Jerusalem.

Setting: In Mark there is only an empty tomb while in Matthew, Luke, and John there are specific appearances of the resurrected Jesus to disciples and followers.

Recognition: In Matthew both women who initially meet the resurrected Jesus near the tomb seem to recognize him immediately and worship him. Later in Matthew, when the resurrected Jesus appears to the disciples in Galilee, they also seem to recognize him immediately, and they, too, worship him. In Luke, the two men who are walking to Emmaus do not recognize the risen Jesus. It is only in the breaking of bread that they finally appear to know who he is. Later in Luke when Jesus appears to the disciples, they think they are seeing a ghost. Only after he invites them to look at his hands and feet and after he eats a piece of fish with them do they seem to fully recognize him. In John we have an account of Mary Magdalene being addressed by the resurrected Jesus, "Woman, why are you crying? Who is it that you are looking for?" Obviously there is no recognition on her part.

Presence: The Gospel narratives also record various ways of portraying and describing the resurrected presence of Jesus. In John 20:19, the resurrected Jesus is one who is able to move through locked doors like a spirit, implying a radically transformed presence completely unlike his earthly presence. In that same passage we also are told the disciples are invited to touch Jesus' hands and side, suggesting a presence that is similar to his earthly presence. In Luke, the resurrected Jesus eats a piece of fish and breaks bread, yet he appears to the disciples like a ghost, disappearing from their sight in the road to Emmaus story.

Women: The Gospels vary in their reporting of the women who went to the tomb. In Mark, Mary Magdalene and Mary, the mother of James and Salome, are present. In Matthew, it is Mary Magdalene and "the other Mary." In Luke, it is Mary Magdalene and Joanna and Mary, the mother of James, and the other women with them. In John, Mary Magdalene alone is present.

Angels: The descriptions of the angels at the tomb vary in the Gospels. In Matthew an angel from heaven comes and rolls back the stone. The angel is sitting on the stone when the women arrive. This angel's appearance is like lightning; he is clothed in garments as white as stone. He speaks to the women at the tomb telling them to not be afraid and then shows them the empty tomb and commissions them to go and tell the other disciples. In Mark, the angel is dressed in a white robe and is inside the tomb instead of sitting on the rolled back stone. In Luke, the angels appear as two men in dazzling clothes standing beside them in the tomb. They ask the women, "Why do you look for the living among the dead?" In John, there are two angels as in Luke, but they are sitting where the body of Jesus had been lying and they ask Mary Magdalene why she is weeping. In this Gospel, it is Jesus who commissions Mary to tell the other disciples, not the angels.

Scholarship: Not only are there great differences among the Gospel narratives themselves, there are even more differences in how scholars interpret these differences. For instance, some scholars believe there were private appearances, such as the appearance to Mary Magdalene or the appearances to the two on the road to Emmaus, as well as official, more public appearances[3] including the appearances to the disciples as a group and to the large crowd to which Paul refers in I Corinthians 15:6. There are many other scholars who would not make those distinctions at all. Some scholars believe that the risen Christ's appearance to Peter was far more important than the appearances to the women, while other scholars believe that appearances to the women are central and primary, indicating a strong historical foundation.[4]

These are only a few of the differences that exist in the New Testament accounts of the resurrection and how those accounts are interpreted. They are differences and discrepancies that are utterly understandable if you read the Gospels as narrative accounts rather than as documented factual history. It is not that the historical details surrounding Jesus' resurrection are insignificant to the authors. The accounts they share certainly have taken actual historical experiences seriously. It is simply that conveying historical information is not their primary concern. Their fundamental priority is how to make the resurrection of Jesus accessible and available to the communities of faith of which they are a part and how to make the resurrection of Jesus real and vital to communities of people who did not witness it directly. Their concern is how to encourage and empower communities of faith to proclaim and embody this resurrection power in their own lives in the world.

Proclaiming an Enduring Legacy of Faith

The homiletical challenge surrounding this primary concern of the Gospel writers is a very serious one. How can we as preachers proclaim a similar passionate and enduring legacy of faith in our own religious communities? Will our resurrection preaching be so contextual, so vibrant, so convincing, so intentional, so responsive to the people's needs that it will make the presence of the resurrected Jesus believable, accessible, and available? And just as the Gospel narratives were focused on Jesus' resurrection, they also knew that this event, this experience, was ultimately about the power of God and God's action in the world. We do not preach only to make a historical Jesus somehow mystically present today. We preach resurrected Jesus because in that normative, central event of the Christian faith we have been given words, stories, and experiences of hope and promise. These stories provide language and meaning in order that we might claim for the first time, or rekindle again, the power of God's resurrection in our own lives and in the communities of faith in which we live.

Francis Schüssler Fiorenza simply says, "Christian faith proclaims the resurrection of Jesus both as a singular event in history and as an event with universal significance."[5] We proclaim the resurrection of Jesus, and we proclaim the ongoing power of resurrection in our individual and collective lives. All of this is the task of faith, not the task of historical reporting.

David Buttrick, in talking about the way we as preachers still find ourselves dealing with the resurrection of Jesus as past history rather than present and future promise, writes:

> On Easter Day we preach as if we were handing out facts from the past. . . . But stop and think: In our preaching are we inadvertently

reversing the mind of the first Christian witnesses? The first Christians did not look to the past but to the future. They understood the resurrection in the light of God's promises.[6]

Out of their own religious tradition, those early believers understood Jesus' resurrection as a part of God's salvific action in their history, and many believed this marked the beginning of God's reign, God's new era, and the world breaking in around them.

When we preach the New Testament testimonies as if they were historical accounts, we rob our preaching of power in two distinct ways: First, we trap the resurrection of Jesus and its power in the past; and second, we offer the resurrection narratives as factual reports to be passively received rather than as timeless testimonies ready to engage our own contemporary lives in ways that promise to change our individual and social realities. When we preach the resurrection accounts solely as if they convey literal history, are we not betraying our own faith? Are we not trapped in an apologetic mode ourselves, believing that somehow all of us still need to be convinced that Jesus' resurrection is real and that what will make it real and true is historical fact? In contrast, when we preach the resurrection accounts as testimonies of faith, we are in the realm of proclamation, not persuasion; the realm of present and future hope, not past accomplishment.

Kenan Osborne, in his recent book on the resurrection, affirms the complexity of Jesus' resurrection and the need for preachers and communities of faith to move beyond the purely historical questions of religious meaning. Early in the book Osborne summarizes another scholar's work on the resurrection, a summary that opens up a fuller meaning of the resurrection of Jesus well beyond its historical significance. Osborne restates the categories of meaning in terms of questions:

❖   The historical question: What actually happened?
❖   The soteriological question: How are we saved?
❖   The eschatological question: In what do we hope?
❖   The kerygmatic or ecclesiological question: What do we preach?
❖   The anthropological question: Who is a person of Christian faith? [7]

To preach the resurrection accounts primarily or exclusively as history robs the resurrection of its fullest, salvific meaning for human life and relegates it to only one small aspect of Christian faith, that of the historical. Perhaps this is why the Gospel narratives give no indication that the fact of the empty tomb changed or transformed any of Jesus' early followers.[8] One does not experience resurrection life because a corpse is missing. One experiences resurrection life because something is present, and this presence is what is saving and transforming. Osborne says, "Resurrection faith is not fundamentally faith in an empty tomb. It is faith in the action of God."[9] Radical gospel invites us to move from being preachers who grasp at proof to preachers who reclaim the resurrection of Jesus as that which demonstrates and manifests the life-giving, transformative, resurrecting power and action of God. It is not happenstance that even though Paul develops a very detailed theology of resurrection and believes it is central and primary to faith, he makes no reference to the empty tomb. He does, however, in I Corinthians 15:1–11, proclaim that the risen Christ appeared to Cephas, then to the twelve, then to five hundred brothers and sisters, then to James, then to all the apostles, then finally to Paul himself. It is not an empty tomb and the absence of a body that is critical to Paul's theology and faith, rather it is the living presence of the Risen Christ.

> The second homiletical challenge that rises from reclaiming radical gospel is the challenge of preaching in ways that are truthful about the risk and terror of resurrection.

All the way through the Gospel accounts of Jesus' resurrection, we find his disciples and followers silent, disbelieving, afraid. The interpretation of this fear as unfaithfulness by preachers throughout the decades is a homiletical travesty. Only the privileged, or those utterly untouched by human violence and murder, would preach in a way that is this abstracted from the concrete realities surrounding those early followers.

Marianne Sawicki invites us into the truth of what it must have actually felt like for those early followers and why it is so important to be truthful about their reality:

> The community was grief-stricken, the women were wailing. It was awful; and if you haven't lost someone you love to a violent death, then you can't even begin to understand what it was like. Sixty years afterward, the churches had four sanitized little stories about a trip to a garden and a lovely surprise. But it wasn't like that when it happened.[10]

Sawicki rightfully draws us back from our potential abstractions into the concrete realities of grief and fear for those early followers. She even suggests that perhaps this grief and fear were a part of what enabled them to discern or perceive, experience, and believe the resurrection.

Yet, are the Gospel accounts only sanitized little stories? I do not think so. People in the early Jesus movement were persecuted and marginalized. They were forced to engage in acts of explaining and defending who they were and why they continued to follow and embody the work and ministry of one who died in such a scandalous way on a political cross. The fact that the authors of the Gospels acknowledge and preserve so many experiences of silence, fear, and disbelief is remarkable and radical. The authors of the Gospels did not forget the reality of crucifixion nearly as readily as we do. The authors of the Gospels clearly remembered that resurrection comes into the very midst of death and destruction in ways that we would like to deny.

❖   Mark 16:8 reads, "So they went out and fled from the tomb, for terror and amazement had seized them; and they said nothing to anyone, for they were afraid."

❖   In Matthew 28:8–17, fear is real and palpable. "So they departed quickly from the tomb with fear and great joy, and ran to tell the disciples. . . . Then Jesus said to them, 'Do not be afraid; go and tell my followers to go to Galilee, and there they will see me.' . . . Now the eleven disciples went to Galilee, to the mountain to which Jesus had directed them. And when they saw Jesus, they worshiped Jesus; but some doubted."

❖   In Luke 24:5, we read, "The women were terrified and bowed their faces to the ground, but the men said to them, 'Why do you look for the living among the dead? He is not here, but has risen.'" After the women witness to the disciples, verse 11 reads, "But these words seemed to them an idle tale, and they did not believe them." Verses 36–43 read, "While they were talking about this, Jesus himself stood among them and said to them, 'Peace be with you.' They were startled and terrified, and thought that they were seeing a ghost. He said to them, 'Why are you frightened, and why do doubts arise in your hearts? Look at my hands and my feet; see that it is I myself. Touch me and see; for a ghost does not have flesh and bones as you see that I have.' And when he had said this, he showed them his hands and his feet. While in joy they were disbelieving and still wondering, he said to them, 'Have you anything here to eat?' They gave him a piece of broiled fish, and he took it and ate in their presence."

❖   In John, Mary is weeping because Jesus' body is not in the tomb; the disciples are behind closed, locked doors because they are afraid; Thomas does not instantly believe; the disciples do not know Jesus as he stands on the beach; and Peter must be asked three times if he loves Jesus.

In terms of defending their own actions and their own beliefs to a world that would make a mockery of them and the Jesus they followed, the authors would have had every reason to leave these descriptions of fear, terror, disbelief, and silence out of their accounts; yet they did not. I think they did not leave these descriptions out because the compelling truthfulness about Jesus' resurrection in particular, and God's resurrecting power in general, would not let them. They were not experiencing uncomplicated joy and glory. They were not experiencing triumphal victory. They were not experiencing doubtless, unwavering faith. They were experiencing resurrection—the abiding resurrected presence of Jesus among them, a God-given power and presence that was raising them up into new ways of being human, new ways of being religious community, new ways of witnessing to the power of life and justice in the larger world. And in the midst of all this life, there were still moments of silence, disbelief, and terror. Again, only people of privilege who are sheltered from the life and death paradoxes of daily existence would be surprised by these simultaneous affirmations.

C. S. Song describes this interwoven reality of life and death well:

> Life is pronounced in the world seized by death. Resurrection is declared from the very place terrorized by death. Jesus' message of life does not come from a paradise that knows no death. It comes from within the world threatened and tyrannized by death.[11]

Radical gospel proclaims resurrection in the midst of death, terror, disbelief, and silence. It preserves the unmitigated paradox of resurrection and refuses to simplify its complexity, refuses to detach it from crucifixion and death, refuses to hide its terrifying demands and joys. Let us embrace the homiletical challenge posed to us by this radical gospel by being preachers who also refuse to proclaim these testimonies of Jesus' resurrection as "sanitized little stories about a trip to a garden and a lovely surprise."

> The third homiletical challenge that rises from reclaiming radical gospel is the challenge of proclaiming the original vision of the reign of God, of which the resurrection is a fundamental part.

In reading the Gospel accounts of Jesus' resurrection, one is quickly confronted with the reality that individual resurrection and eternal life are not the primary focus of the authors' proclamations. In Jewish apocalyptic thought, Jesus' resurrection would have been understood as inseparably intertwined with a communal resurrection at the end of time as "the Jews as a whole believed that on the last day the dead would rise again."[12] Both in the Gospels and in the writings of Paul, resurrection would have been understood in a larger, cosmic context of the end times, the parousia, the beginning of the reign of God, all of which were images of God's transforming action that had implications for all creation, not for an isolated individual. Jesus' resurrection would have been understood and experienced within this theological framework, which is precisely what led many to believe the world as they knew it was coming to an end. This image of resurrection was about God's judgment and ultimate reign; it was not about personal eternal life since in "the life, death, and resurrection of Jesus Christ, God has begun to concretely realize what was expected to take place at the end of time: to establish justice and to struggle against the powers of death."[13] It was that end time and God's reign of justice and God's victory over death that were at stake in the resurrection, not personal and individual immortality.

Even though Jesus' resurrection was interpreted in complex and varied ways in relation to Jewish apocalyptic thought, I am persuaded that his resurrection is fundamentally related to the reign of God he preached throughout his life and ministry. Jesus' resurrection, then, is radically consistent with his life, ministry, and crucifixion. He preached the reign of God, and that reign of God for Jesus had to do with a new humanity and a transformed world order. His message was social from beginning to end. No less social is the message and reality of his resurrection.

It is not possible to fully grasp the social and communal nature of Jesus' resurrection without an equally full understanding of the reign of God, the vision Jesus preached, and the vision for which Jesus died. Any preaching ministry faithful and responsive to the radical gospel of Jesus must come to grips with the reign of God he preached and the relationship of this reign to his resurrection. Osborne says, "The central theme of Jesus' risen message is the kingdom of God which is exactly the same as the central theme of Jesus' preaching during his earthly life."[14]

The reign of God is that vision of a transformed, just world that is the horizon of all my preaching and the horizon of my Christian faith. Jesus' life, ministry, and preaching concretized what that reign of God looks like. It looks like fathers throwing parties for sons who were lost and have been found. It looks like laborers working different hours and being paid the same wages. It looks like tax collectors being held accountable and being offered new life. It looks like being neighbor to the stranger. It looks like people placing their lives beside the oppressed and marginalized and resisting the violences done to them even if that leads to a murderous cross. It looks like women being the first ones to proclaim the hope of resurrection.

The Brazilian bishop Pedro Casaldáliga and a Nicaraguan priest, José-María Vigil, say:

> *What was absolute for Jesus was the "Reign of God."* . . . When God reigns, all is changed. . . . The Reign of God is the total overturning and transfiguring of the present condition of ourselves and the cosmos, purified from all evils and filled with the condition of God.[15]

The reign of God is that overarching vision toward which Christian life must move, what God desires and promises. Resurrection is the power, the experience, and the historical and the embodied reality that tell me that this reign is possible and that we can taste it in this lifetime. Resurrection is God's limitless ability to raise up life in the midst of every conceivable death. Resurrection is the assurance, the hope, the promise that God, with human agency, can bring about new life, that life can prevail, and that justice can be realized. For me as a Christian preacher, without the concrete experience of resurrection, the vision of the reign of God would seem utterly romantic, abstract, impossible, illusionary, and hopeless. We use the word resurrection to point to those concrete moments and experiences that are a part of the reign of God. The experiences are on the way to the full and complete reality of the reign of God, the process we must undergo, a foretaste, a touch, a partial glimpse of the ultimate promise of God's transformative life. C. S. Song says, "The Resurrection is essentially the proclamation that the reign of God is here, that it is in the midst of us in the world."[16] We use the word "resurrection" to remind ourselves as a Christian community that God's power is not, and will never be, ultimately controlled or silenced by the forces of violence, injustice, and death. This understanding of resurrection is what is at the heart of the Gospel accounts. It is social and political in nature, for it is about a transformed humanity and a transformed world.

Throughout this book, we have been reminding ourselves that every theological concept and understanding must be contextualized. The reign of God is one of the terms which also needs to be put in context in order for us to best understand its meaning.

Juan Luis Segundo's work on the reign of God is enormously helpful and challenging. He believes that when Jesus spoke about the kingdom of God, he spoke three distinct messages, each pertaining to a distinct listening audience. Some of what he said about the kingdom of God was intended for the religious and political leaders of his day, those who had power and those who were in a position of oppressing and marginalizing others. Some of what he said about the kingdom or reign of God was intended for the disciples who closely followed his ministry and were a part of it. Some of what he said about the kingdom or reign of God was intended for the poor and oppressed, the marginalized, and outcast.[17] Segundo clearly states what is at the heart of these distinctive messages:

> The Kingdom of God is not announced to everyone. It is not "proclaimed" to all. That is not due to a decision made by Jesus; it is due to the very essence of the kingdom. It is not so much that Jesus establishes differences so that he gets a hearing from some and not from others ... Far more important is the fact that the kingdom itself cannot be preached indiscriminately as good news, as gospel. The kingdom is destined for certain groups. It is theirs. It belongs to them. Only for them will it be a cause for joy. And, according to Jesus, the dividing line between joy and woe, produced by the kingdom runs between the poor and the rich.[18]

The poor and oppressed will hear Jesus' words about the reign of God as a joyful announcement, words that herald a new and transformed world filled with justice and right relations. The powerful and those who oppress will hear Jesus' words about the reign of God as a message of terror and woe, words that threaten the present world order, filled with loss and indictment. Those who follow in Jesus' way, the disciples, will hear Jesus' words about the reign of God as vocational challenge, words that urge faithful action and call for accountability and vision.

Segundo asserts that there is a basic message embedded in Jesus' proclamations about the kingdom of God for each group of people in Jesus' day. For those who are rich, powerful, and privileged, Jesus' words call for conversion.[19] Those who are powerful must radically change. They must change their worldview, their values, their ethical practices, their lives. The only way they will ever know the reign of God as gospel or good news is if they change their lives so dramatically that they are living side by side with those who are oppressed, those who find the promise of a new heaven and earth their deepest, most passionate desire. For those who are the followers of Jesus' way, Jesus' words call for *prophetism and conscientization* [20] Just as Jesus makes demands on those who have power, Segundo believes he also makes demands on those who would follow in his way:

> The demands are not preconditions for entering the kingdom. . . . Instead Jesus demands certain qualities from them, prophetic qualities that are part and parcel of Jesus' mission. They must display all the clear-sightedness, heroism, and commitment that prophetism implies and that was certainly required of Jesus himself . . .[21]

The disciples must not only display certain courageous behaviors, but they also must come to understand with absolute clarity the social, political, and religious structures and powers of their day. In contemporary language, one might say that Jesus is demanding that they deepen their social, political, and ecclesiastical analysis so that they can better discern and resist the forces of injustice and evil that surround them. Until they raise their consciousness about the world in which they live and the realities that shape that world, privileging some and enslaving and oppressing others, they will be ineffective as those who proclaim and embody God's new humanity, God's transformed creation.

And finally, for those who make up the third group: sinners, the poor and oppressed, Jesus' words call for *acceptance and belief.* They are the recipients of the good news. This is not an easy or natural call. Segundo reminds us: "But the poor themselves are also in need of a certain change of outlook or conversion so that they may *believe* in the good news, precisely because it is *so good,* so seemingly incredible, and so different from their accustomed situation."[22] In contemporary language again, we might describe this as Jesus' inviting those who are poor and oppressed to understand that they are not simply victims, but moral and ethical agents. It might also involve enabling those who have lost all hope to feel and to know hope and promise again.

In light of Segundo's work, the homiletical challenge, related to the reign of God that was at the heart of Jesus' resurrection, is great. We need to recover Jesus' vision of the reign of God in ways that are appropriate and faithful to our particular religious communities and social contexts. Are we preaching in contexts that require us to preach radical conversion and relinquishment in order to faithfully participate in building and embodying the reign of God? Are we preaching in contexts that require us to preach courageous prophetic action in the world in order to empower the building and embodying of the reign of God? Are we preaching in contexts that require us to invite and urge those who are without hope to hope again? Are we preaching in contexts where we need to invite those who are the most oppressed to realize and claim there is a radical, transformative message in Christianity worthy of their belief and investment?

What Jesus' teaching and preaching confront us with is that there is no generic message about the reign of God. We must contextualize it and, in so doing, discover the radical message that is ours to preach.

> The fourth homiletical challenge that rises from reclaiming radical gospel is to allow that vision of the reign of God to reshape and reconfirm the church's mission in the world.

It is not enough to simply preach about the reign of God as ultimate vision of a transformed world and resurrection as concrete taste or glimpse of that new world. This is the vision that Jesus lived, preached, and embodied in the resurrection. This vision makes a claim upon our individual lives as Christian people and certainly makes claims on the Christian church as a whole. Francis Schüssler Fiorenza clearly links the resurrection to the mission of the whole Christian church:

Belief in the resurrection of Jesus entails a vision of reality, a vision of the presence of God's power, that not only illumines the life and faith of Jesus but also grounds the mission of the Church. This vision gives new meaning to Jesus' life and at the same time provides a meaning for the Church and its mission—as the Gospel accounts make evident.[23]

Even though it is clear the church's mission is at stake in the resurrection of Jesus, just as the church's mission is related to others aspects of the Gospel accounts, there is no uniform way of understanding this mission. Let me make a few observations about the church's mission that arise from the Gospels.

❖   In Mark 16:6, 7, these words are spoken to the women at the tomb by the young man wearing a white robe: "Don't be alarmed. I know you are looking for Jesus of Nazareth, who was nailed to the cross. He is not here—he has been raised! Now go and give this message to his disciples, including Peter: He is going to Galilee ahead of you; there you will see him, just as he told you."

❖   The women are sent out from the tomb to proclaim the

resurrection to the disciples. This sending out is from Jerusalem, and it is significant that Mark portrays the women still in the city. They have not fled throughout the crucifixion and the days following, and they have come to the tomb to anoint the body. At this point in the Gospel story, many scholars believe Mark portrays the women's faithfulness in contrast to the men. Perhaps because of this faithfulness in the face of terror and grief, they are now in position to be the ones instructed with the mission of being witnesses to Jesus' resurrection. Yet, the final verse of Mark reminds us that the women left the tomb and said nothing to anyone, because they were afraid. Even though there are many interpretations of this abrupt ending to the Gospel of Mark, and no ultimate decisive conclusions, the abruptness opens up the notion of mission in incredible and poignant ways. Perhaps Mark is saying that be-cause the male disciples fled, and the female disciples were silent, it is the early church community, and the church community throughout the ages, that must assume the mission of bearing witness to the resurrection. Robert Smith affirms the positive and challenging dimensions of Mark's ending:

> Mark has concluded his gospel hopefully and mysteriously. His ending has the effect of throwing the readers back upon themselves, placing them in the position of having to make a decision for or against "Jesus and Galilee," and that means for or against discipleship and ministry, for or against different kinds of futures for themselves.[24]

The responsibility of that mission has a timeless quality to it because of Mark's ending and a more universal challenge to every Christian person reading it and hearing it proclaimed.

In Matthew 28:5–7, we read:

> The angel spoke to the women. "You must not be afraid," he said. "I know you are looking for Jesus, who was nailed to the cross. He is not here; he has been raised, just as he said. Come here and see the place where he lay. Quickly, now, go and tell his disciples, 'He has been raised from death, and now he is going to Galilee ahead of you; there you will see him!' Remember what I have told you."

The women in Matthew's Gospel are not silent, rather they are described as leaving the grave in a hurry filled with joy and running to tell the disciples the very message they have been given.

In that same Gospel, when the disciples see Jesus in Galilee they worship him, then Jesus instructs them in verse 19: "Go, therefore, and make disciples of all nations, baptizing them in the name of God the Father and Mother, and of Jesus Christ the beloved Child, and of the Holy Spirit, teaching them to observe all that I have commanded you; and I am with you always, to the close of the age."

Kenan Osborne lifts up and reflects upon the specific message and mission given to the women at the tomb in these words:

> The social or public aspect of Easter is evident. The appearance was not a private vision simply for the devotion and edification of the women involved. The women, as loyal disciples of Jesus, have been entrusted with a message of reconciliation, that is: even though the male disciples had fled and some had even rejected Jesus, Jesus now takes the initiative to meet them in Galilee and thus be reconciled with them.[25]

Osborne, drawing upon the work of many biblical scholars, believes the first part of the mission for early followers in Matthew's religious community centered around reconciliation. The women are clearly called to be agents of this reconciling ministry between Jesus and the disciples.

Where is reconciliation needed, and who are to be the bearers of that reconciliation? The women were to help reconcile Jesus with the disciples who had fled, denied him, and abandoned him. Perhaps the radical message the contemporary church might hear in this for its own life is that we are precisely the ones who have compromised and abandoned the radical social mandates of the reign of God which Jesus proclaimed, that we are the ones who deny and flee. In criticizing the church as having greatly reduced and compromised Jesus' radical message, David Buttrick says, "So let us promise a heart transformation and leave the social order alone. All that exaggerated stuff about God's new order must be regarded as a first-century aberration and not central to the gospel of love."[26] Who will bring resurrection life to the contemporary church and call it back to Jesus' vision of the reign of God? Who will take up the mission of the women and bring a world of reconciliation and accountability to the church of Jesus Christ today?

What does it mean to preach, to proclaim the resurrected Jesus in a world filled with death and violence and, in the face of all kinds of social and ecclesiastical imperialism, what will it look like to make disciples? We need to be cautious as we preach these mission challenges. We hear them and perceive them from contexts of institutionalized churches and from within communities of firm Christian identity, but this was not the situation in which Matthew's Gospel was experienced. Perhaps in an emerging, fledgling religious community, making disciples meant being witness to the resurrection, embodying aspects of the just reign of God to those who were under foreign occupation, and reassuring new believers of God's sustaining power. Perhaps as preachers, the only way we can rediscover the radical dimensions of Matthew's Gospel is to remember once again that Jesus was calling for participation in resurrection and in God's ultimate reign of love and justice. He was not calling for more institutional members, nor was he urging religious imperialism.

Luke 24:45–49 reads,

> Then Jesus opened their minds to understand the Scriptures, and said to them, "Thus it is written, that the Messiah should suffer and on the third day rise from the dead, and that repentance and forgiveness of sins should be preached in the Messiah's name to all nations, beginning from Jerusalem. You are witnesses of these things. And I am sending the promise of God my Father and Mother upon you; but stay in the city until you are clothed with power from on high."

This message would have been heard by Luke's community as Jesus' interpreting the Jewish scriptures; connecting his own life, ministry, and death to those scriptures; and giving the disciples instructions for their future work in the world. They were to be witnesses to the resurrection and to the coming of God's new reign, and they are to wait in Jerusalem until the power of the spirit came upon them. Perhaps the visionary challenge in relation to the mission of the disciples and ultimately the church has to do with the inclusivity of that mission. They are to begin witnessing to the resurrection and the reign of God in Jerusalem, a place of occupied power, the very place Jesus was killed. Yet this is only a beginning to their mission. They are commissioned to move into all the world as witnesses.

Once again, it would be too easy and far too institutionalized to assume that Luke intends his community to hear their commissioning from Jesus as a mandate to convert all the world to a certain religion, to Christianity. These are Jews who are instructed to bear witness to the resurrection and to God's new age to other Jews and to Gentiles. We would do well to proclaim this as an ongoing challenge to the contemporary church to bear witness to the reign of God to other Christians, to see this as an act of internal religious witnessing, and to discern what bearing witness to a new humanity and a new age looks like to those unlikely to experience that good news, unlikely to feel included in it, and unlikely to be the recipient of God's greatest gift.

In John 20:17, after an encounter between Mary Magdalene and the risen Jesus, he said to her, "Do not hold me, for I have not yet ascended to God; but go to my friends and say to them, 'I am ascending to God my Father and Mother and your Father and Mother, to my God and your God.'" Here Mary receives the commissioning, and in John's Gospel it centers around telling his followers that he will be exalted with God. For John and his community, this was an important theological message and affirmation. Perhaps a great challenge to the mission of the church is to proclaim and embody a gospel where all people truly are friends. This is not some romanticized notion of friends, for Jesus clearly calls those who have the courage and perseverance to follow in his ways friends. This intimate new identity with Jesus and with one another is the centerpiece of God's new age. The church would do well to discover anew what this really looks like in our alienated and violent world.

And another powerful challenge to the church's mission comes in the next section of John where the disciples are gathered behind closed doors for fear. There is no direct commissioning given to the disciples here, but the implication certainly is that they must learn how to survive and to proclaim the resurrection in the midst of hostility and persecution. Since in North America most of the Christian church does not experience this kind of political and ecclesiastical persecution, it is more difficult for us to know our comparable mission. Perhaps we need to start by asking ourselves why the church in North America feels no fear.

Some of Archbishop Oscar Romero's most prophetic and challenging words spoke to just this issue:

> I rejoice, brothers and sisters, that our church is persecuted precisely for its preferential option for the poor, and for seeking to become incarnate in the interests of the poor. . . . How sad it would be, in a country where such horrible murders are being committed, if there were no priests among the victims! A murdered priest is a testimonial of a church incarnate in the problems of the people.[27]

What mission would the church need to take up, and about what mission would we need to preach, that would actually make us fearful? Where is the Christian church in North America choosing a preferential option for the victims of injustice so persistently its leaders are threatened and persecuted?

Even though scholars differ in their interpretations of these appear-ance narratives, many would agree that there is some kind of commis-sioning that is given by the resurrected Jesus to those who experience his appearance. These appearances have often been interpreted, as are the empty tomb portions of the narratives, as proofs of the truth that Jesus has been resurrected. Francis Fiorenza believes the appearances are firmly connected to the issues of Jesus' identity and the church's mission in the world:

> Matthew's description of the commissioning underscores the power and presence of the Risen Lord in the Church as ground of its universal mission. Since Luke associates apostleship with witness to the resurrection, he has the appearances stretch out over a longer period of time. The Risen Lord opens the meaning of the Scriptures and establishes the Church so that a new stage of salvation history begins. John's Gospel relates the commissioning to the forgiveness of sin.
>
> The combination of the motifs of commissioning and identity show that the basic goal of the appearance stories is not to prove the resurrection of Jesus but to show the link between the Church's mission and the historical Jesus. The identity of the Risen Lord with the historical Jesus is the key to the appearance stories.[28]

May we in preaching these resurrection narratives renew the church's mission. May we preach a radical commissioning to the contemporary followers of Jesus that actually makes us fearful. And let us rediscover once again that the church's fundamental mission is to proclaim and embody glimpses of the reign of God until such a day and time when all creation will know it fully.

Reclaiming the Gospel accounts of the resurrection as testimonies of faith, not historical documents; being truthful about the risk and terror of resurrection; recommitting our lives and preaching to the reign of God of which the resurrection is a fundamental part; and reshaping and rediscovering the church's radical mission in the world as those who are called to embody that reign of God now: These are the challenges of reclaiming the radical gospel at the heart of the resurrec-tion narratives.

Let us proclaim these Gospel narratives, seeking to hear them, feel them, live them anew. Let us probe these texts and struggle with them, knowing that on the other side of resurrection there is always a call, a commissioning, a sending forth, a mission. And let us remember that in every case, those who were sent out or commissioned by the resur-rected Jesus were sent out even though they did not fully understand, even though they were disbelieving, even though they were afraid.

SERMON

RESURRECTION—CALLED FORTH FROM PLACES OF HIDING

Read John 20:19–29

Hear these challenging words from Jack Pantaleo reflecting on the death and resurrection of Jesus:

> In the life of Christ, we encounter this ultimate sacrifice. Jesus, as we all know, sacrificed his life. Nailed to a cross and crucified, he gave up his very life, echoing his own words that one can have no greater love than to give up one's life for a friend.
>
> What an extraordinary sacrifice that was! Yet it was not the ultimate sacrifice, for if Jesus had stopped there, he would be remembered only as another nice teacher who spoke about love.
>
> Let's face it: death had been done before. Anyone can die. Jesus revolutionized creation because he had the nerve it took not to remain dead. Christ went beyond sacrificing his life. He sacrificed his death. He voluntarily let go of the comfort of death and fought to rise above the grave.
>
> The hardest thing we can do is not to die, but to live, and to live abundantly in joy.[29]

It is no coincidence that a gay man describes resurrection as a sacrifice of death—voluntarily letting go of the comfort of death. Pantaleo writes these words because he knows something very profound about closets, hiding places, locked doors: those places that give needed security and protection, yet are ultimately places of stifling, suffocation, death. He also knows something deep and hopeful about fighting to rise above the grave, for he writes these words shortly after a time in his life when he was brutally raped by a stranger. He is struggling for his life. He is fighting to rise above the grave. He is determined to sacrifice the dimensions of death that keep him from the promise and possibility of life.

What an extraordinary image of resurrection: the act of sacrificing death. Jesus has been spit on and mocked. He has been betrayed by loved ones and misunderstood by friends. He has been broken to the point of wondering if God has forsaken him and, finally, tortured and murdered. In the face of this, death might just be a blessed ending. But Jesus sacrifices the comfort of death to return for a time to those he loves. He appears to his disciples and friends, not just to reassure and console. He appears to them to call them forth from their places of hiding back into the world. He comes asking them to voluntarily let go of the comforts of denial, escape, closed doors, and to live, to live abundantly in joy.

"When it was evening on that day, the first day of the week, the doors of the house where the disciples had met were locked for fear. . . ."

Fear is a powerful and strange thing in our lives. It prompts us to seek protection in times of very real danger. It motivates us into needed changes and surprising adventures. It serves as constant reminder that we are fragile, limited, human. In contrast to these life-giving impulses of fear, we know fear can also immobilize us, cause us to "lock the doors" of our lives, and run away from life into places of isolated hiding.

Very few human emotions are as strong as fear. Very few experiences are as overwhelming and disorienting as those moments in life when we feel genuinely afraid. These early followers of Jesus are hiding for good reason. They are afraid. They have seen Jesus brutally murdered and were helpless to stop it. They know they could be next. It would be reasonable to expect Jesus to encourage them to get out of Jerusalem and hide anywhere they could. But no, he does not just come to call them forth. He comes to tell them to feed and tend all God's people, to preach the gospel to the whole creation, and to receive the power of the Holy Spirit.

His mandates are relentless, even after his death. The disciples cannot escape them. Even in the midst of being terrified and lost, even in the midst of their reasonable, justifiable fear, he calls them to abundant life. Jesus sacrifices the comfort of his own death, and he commissions them to do the same. He calls them to open the doors of their lives and to come forth from their places of hiding.

Jesus comes as absolute assurance that the power of God that has raised him right up out of the grave will be with them also. It is the greatest assurance and the greatest promise he can possibly give them.

Why, after he appears as the resurrected one to some of the disciples in this place of hiding, are they still in that same place of hiding eight days later? Resurrection life, life that leaves tombs empty and grave clothes undone, is not always such a glorious and joyful thing. Resurrection life, life that speaks our name and commissions us to speak its power to others, is rarely embraced by us with abandonment. Resurrection life, life that holds out wounded hands and pierced bodies and invites us to see and touch, is seldom what we would boldly choose.

It should not surprise us that Julia Esquivel, a poet who has known more violent deaths in her lifetime than most of us can imagine, speaks about being "threatened with Resurrection." If resurrection has to do with sacrificing death, unlocking all the closed doors of our lives, then most of us have reason to feel threatened. If resurrection has to do with having the nerve it takes not to remain dead and fighting to rise above every kind of grave, then it should not be difficult for most of us to clearly understand why the disciples are hiding eight days later. There are so many forms of death and so many graves to rise above.

The mystery and gift of resurrection is that, although it cannot be fully understood or possessed, it is utterly tangible. The disciples are not transformed by some intellectual notion of resurrection. Their lives are changed by the concrete reality of the presence of Jesus among them. I find it strange that so many interpretations of this particular resurrection story over the years have named it a story about doubting Thomas because of his need for tangible signs of Jesus' resurrected presence. Thomas simply asks to experience what Jesus has so freely given to the others. Jesus knows that in the days and years ahead they will need the power of resurrection to face the forces that will threaten them with silence and death.

The more I think about the courage that is required of us to face the claims and expectations of resurrection life, the more admiration I gain for Thomas. It is true he wanted and needed to see Jesus' hands and side. Who of us would not have needed this same reassurance? I can relate readily to his need.

What is amazing and somewhat shocking are Thomas's words: "Unless I see the mark of the nails in his hands, and put my finger in the mark of the nails and my hand in his side, I will not believe." Unlike the other disciples who simply see, Thomas longs to come close, to embrace, to touch. Thomas knows his own human limitations and boldly asks for what he needs. Maybe he knows that once he comes this close, he will never be the same.

I wonder what would change in our world if more of us were willing to put our fingers in the mark of the nails that crucify people daily and put our hands in broken and wounded sides? Resurrection life can be so palpable, so real, it promises to change us forever. Jesus does not condemn Thomas. He simply says, "Have you believed because you have seen me? Blessed are those who have not seen and yet have come to believe."

Is it not the same for us? Does it not take a human face, a particular voice, a concrete need to compel us to sacrifice the comforts of death, the graves of denial, apathy, isolation, and to move us closer toward abundant life?

Oscar Romero, archbishop of El Salvador, was moved toward resurrection by the lives and faces of his own people. Their brutal repression just kept finding him despite the locked doors of the church hierarchy and the hiding he tried so hard to do.

Dorothy Day, founder of the Catholic Worker movement, was moved toward resurrection by the homeless and hungry on the streets of New York City who were only asking for a simple meal, a place to rest, and some small portion of hospitality.

Daniel Berrigan, priest of peace, was moved toward resurrection by the images of an annihilated world and the destruction of all our children, both of which compelled him into civil disobedience against the production of nuclear weapons.

AIDS activists in ACT UP are moved toward resurrection by the ravaged bodies of loved ones and the community's valuing of life. Both things drive them into the streets and churches to demonstrate against a system that appears so indifferent to human life.

Welfare rights advocates are moved toward resurrection as they stand side by side with protesting single mothers who work and still have hungry children. They are moved toward resurrection as they stand shoulder to shoulder with African American men who work full time and cannot pay their rent.

Resurrection is not just something that happens to us after we leave this life as we know it. Resurrection is something that happens in profound ways in our everyday lives. It is not something that only comes at the end of Lent, at the end of struggle and death, but it can come and does come in the very midst of it.

Yet let us not protest that people experience resurrection in the same ways. For some of us, the act of "coming forth from places of hiding" will cost us our lives. For others of us, the claim of resurrection life may not be this great; yet, if we are honest, we know that no matter where we live our lives, true resurrection is inseparably linked with death. We wish it would come painlessly and gloriously, but it often comes into our midst with wounded hands and side. And we are afraid to touch, to come closer, to put our hands in the side of its presence.

Joyce Hollyday invites us to come closer and experience the power of resurrection in the lives of women struggling to survive. A few years ago preparations were being made for Christmas in a Salvadoran refugee camp in Honduras. Only days before, national guard members had come to the home of a young catechist, tied him up, and taken him away. At some point he tried to escape, and they killed him instantly. Later, his pregnant wife and five children gathered around his coffin while a candle burned in the darkness.

In another part of the camp, a group of women gathered around a very sick infant. They had sung to him in a dark tent, lit only by the light of a candle. Between the verses of the song, the cries of his mother could be heard filling the air. She had tried to save him by feeding him from an eyedropper, trying to coax some nourishment into his starving body. The child lay among them; he did not cry or move. The child had died.

This was what had happened just before Christmas. But then Christmas Eve came, and the camp burst forth with joy and celebration. The women baked bread while the men butchered pigs for pork tamales. The children created figures for the nativity scene out of clay from the riverbed, adding some of their own special touches to the usual characters: pigs, an armadillo, and baby Jesus sleeping in a hammock. They made ornaments from small medicine boxes and shaped figures from the tinfoil that wraps margarine sticks, and they hung these on a tree branch. The children dressed as shepherds and passed from tent to tent, recounting the journey of "José and María" in search of shelter.

Yvonne Dilling, a church worker from Indiana in the camp, said a refugee woman once asked her why she always looked so sad and burdened. Yvonne talked about the grief she felt over all the suffering she was witnessing and her commitment to give all of herself to the struggle of the refugees. This woman gently confronted her: "Only people who expect to go back to North America in a year work the way you do. You cannot be serious about our struggle unless you play and celebrate and do the things that make it possible to give a lifetime to it."

Every time the refugees were displaced and had to build a new camp, they immediately formed three committees: a construction committee, an education committee, and the *comité de alegría*—the committee of joy. Celebration was as basic to the life of the refugees as digging latrines and teaching their children to read.[30]

Maybe sacrificing death, being called forth from places of hiding, is a lifelong process, a daily process of moving from death toward life.

Maybe resurrection has everything to do with committees of joy in the midst of refugee camps and dying babies, with the brave act of confronting the privileged with the reality of their choice to return at any moment to their comfortable safe lives.

For most of the world, resurrection has more to do with holding on to life, finding life, and creating life in the midst of digging latrines and teaching children to read than it will ever be about glorious, pain-free moments of new life.

O for the privileged of this world to know more clearly, and certainly more passionately, what voluntarily letting go of the comfort of death might look like.

O for all of us to know more fully the graves we live in without even knowing.

O for us to believe in God's power that can radically renew and transform our collective lives.

O for the courage to come forth from places of hiding.

UNTYING GRAVE CLOTHES

In a time when systemic injustice, inflicted suffering, and human despair threaten to overwhelm us, what are we as Christian preachers proclaiming about the power and possibility of resurrection in our contemporary lives? How might our sermons more fully describe and evoke those moments in life when we see, feel, and experience the lived reality of resurrection hope?

In the Christian community, we affirm that Easter is the pinnacle celebration of our faith. The Christian church liturgically remembers and celebrates an entire season called Eastertide, those fifty days between Jesus' resurrection and the coming of the Holy Spirit at Pentecost. At the heart of contemporary liturgical renewal is an effort to reclaim this season as the focal point of the Christian life, an effort to reclaim resurrection as that which we celebrate every time we worship.

Yet, even with renewed liturgical commitments to the resurrection, there are two contradictions that many preachers and communities of faith continue to perpetuate. First, even though we declare Easter to be the heart and soul of the Christian faith, many of our churches treat Eastertide as a less important season than Lent. Perhaps Lent, with the North American Christian church's primary focus on individualized/privatized sin, sacrificial atonement theology, and individualistic spirituality, makes us feel much more comfortable than the deepest challenges of Easter faith do. Why is there this contradiction between what we say is most important and what theologically and liturgically captures most of our attention?

The second contradiction for many of us in the Christian church has to do with the fact that we speak great affirmations about the power and possibility of resurrection, yet rather than embracing its power for our everyday lives, we relegate it exclusively to the mysterious and unknowable dimensions of life beyond this earthly reality, life after bodily death. Also, we reduce it to what distinctly and exclusively happened to Jesus of Nazareth. In the face of all we affirm, why do we have this contradiction about God's resurrecting power? Why do many Christian people continue to understand the power and possibility of resurrection as that which is utterly unavailable to them in their daily lives?

It is my hope that the words that follow will continue to move us toward a greater theological and homiletical emphasis on resurrection in our preaching ministries and will provide significant alternatives to these two contradictions.

Resurrection life has everything to do with investing our lives, committing our lives, placing our lives in all those places where human beings suffer and are oppressed, in all those places where people yearn for new life, for transformed reality, for an experience of resurrection. I believe that Christianity is about forming a people who take the power of resurrection life seriously in their everyday lives and move their bodies and resources into places where that power can bring about new life.

Let us be clear, however: Resurrection as the rising of the dead, or dramatic, vital life experienced on the other side of forms of death, cannot be easily equated with daily rebirth experiences, signs of the earth's reawakening, or experiences of wonder that restore hope and life. These are powerful faith experiences, but perhaps they do not do justice to the distinctive nature of resurrection. Resurrection is inseparably linked with crucifixions and with death. This is why the actual reality of resurrection may be experienced as utterly terrifying as surely as it is celebrative and transformative.

Connections between Lent and Easter

For people who lead privileged lives, the desperate hope and need for Easter and its resurrection power may seem far removed at times. Janet Morley, in *Bread of Tomorrow: Prayers for the Church Year*, opens up the absolute paradox of resurrection when she says:

> Perhaps one of the problems is that we expect Easter to provide an uncomplicated and uncostly sort of joy, and are puzzled when it does not. I take courage from the mood of the gospel resurrection narratives, which on close inspection have a good deal more to say about shock, fear, and a bemused lack of recognition than about immediate delight. It is clear that the disciples, for all their good intentions, found it hard even to see, let alone understand, the earth-shaking change that this "good news" implies. It may be that as the relatively wealthy in this world we both hope for and fear the

changes that the poorest long for and need. And so, to pray at Easter in solidarity with the poor may require us to start from an acknowledgment of our own fear and despair. We pray: "Although we fear change; although we are not ready; although we'd rather weep and run away; Roll Back The Stone."

By contrast, it is those who have literally endured the cost and the risk of Holy Week who are the readiest to hear the message of resurrection and claim it as their truth.[1]

During the season of Lent, perhaps if more preachers and churches placed a greater emphasis on examining and resisting the social and political principalities and powers that crucify and violate people the world over, we would then see churches urgently and passionately turn to the good news of Easter faith. We must be willing to move more fully into the cost and risk of Holy Week with our own lives in order to understand and claim resurrection in new and powerful ways.

I am not speaking here, nor do I think Morley is, of the kind of theological connections between Lent and Easter that suggest suffering and sacrifice are absolutely necessary before one can experience resurrection. Morley is not suggesting what much of traditional sacrificial theology has for centuries: that we must suffer in order to ever know resurrection life. Rather, we must be involved in the work of liberation and salvation in order to know the full power of resurrection in this life. Liberatory and salvific work are the things that are necessary, not suffering. Suffering may be the result of our liberatory work, but it is not what Christians are to seek as an end in itself. We need new ways of talking about the interconnections between Lent and Easter and new ways of proclaiming the fundamental relationship between Lent and Eastertide.

With those few comments about Easter and Lent, let us proceed with the task of re-imaging resurrection as we explore a number of ways that images of resurrection might expand, deepen, and even challenge some of the understandings and images we presently possess.

Images of Resurrection

There is an image from within my own life, and the community of faith of which I am a part, that will begin our exploration.

1. Resurrection as the Body of the Risen Christ/God's Hope for the New Community

When I imagine what a Christian community striving to be the "Body of the Risen Christ" looks like, I imagine my own home church, Spirit of the Lakes United Church of Christ in Minneapolis, Minnesota.

As a church community it was birthed in 1988, as a church that would particularly serve and respond to the lesbian, gay, bisexual, and transgender community. The place of worship is a large warehouse that has been transformed into holy space by all the hungers and hopes people bring. Everywhere I look people are crying. People are crying sometimes out of deep personal loss, sometimes out of passionate connection to the hurts of the world, sometimes out of profound joy and celebration, and many times simply because gay men, lesbian women, bisexual, and transgender people have never known the unity of church, God, love, and sexuality. We sit there as a community, holding each other's longing, and each other's tears, and we seek to turn those tears into rivers of hope.

When we celebrate the eucharist in Christian community, it has the power to constitute us as a people and help us become the Body of the Risen Christ in unspeakably holy ways. Each and every Sunday, these individual Christian men and women, who are marginalized and oppressed by most religious communities around the world, stand in long processional lines waiting to come to the table to partake of the bread of life and the cup of blessing. Yet here is not a weeping or a feasting that is turned inward, but an act that turns us outward into transformative action.

These words are always spoken just before we commune: "Each time we break this bread we participate in the Body of the Risen Christ, for we are the Body of the Risen Christ. And each time we share the cup we participate in the new community, for we are God's hope for the new community."[2]

In these eucharistic moments the meaning and power of anamnesis (the communal act of remembrance) takes on not only meaning for our present lives, but points to the eschatalogical dimensions of this meal as well. As we do these acts of remembering, we not only rehearse the life and ministry of Jesus, but we become a part of the Christic body that becomes anew his life and ministry in the world. This communal act, as traditional and as radical as it is, proclaims and embodies resurrection.

Those who are deemed unacceptable are given the mandate to shape and embody the new community. Those who have seldom been fed by the church are urged and invited to be radical church in the world by feeding others. And after we eat, people are embraced and a blessing is spoken to every individual, every couple, every family, every grouping that so desires. Those who feel condemnation at every turn are offered special blessings. What a dramatic contrast this is to the indicting image of the church painfully offered by Marilyn Alexander and James Preston when they say: "The Church, in silencing the gay and lesbian child of God, makes the Communion rail a prison and the waters of baptism a whirlpool of death because it sends the gay and lesbian out of the Church believing they are less than children of God."[3] At Spirit of the Lakes, gay and lesbian people know they are created sacred by God and that the sacrament of communion is a blessing, not a prison.

What does it mean to be the Body of the Risen Christ?

What does it mean to be a resurrection people? What does it mean for Christian people to passionately breathe life into every place of violence and bravely resist in our neighborhoods, our countrysides, and our cities all the forces that strip people of their humanity and life? What does it mean to be a people who tenderly raise each other up out of tombs of despair and death?

And what does it mean to be God's hope for the new community?

What does it mean to be a visionary people, boldly embodying new ways of being human, and carefully tending places of justice and hope? What does it mean to be a people who courageously forge places of worship and life where everyone has a place at the table, and everyone is blessed?

The images of the *Body of the Risen Christ*, and *God's hope for the new community* are challenging enough; yet something else equally challenging surrounds this depiction of religious community. Are we as preachers, and as faithful Christian people, willing and able to see the ways marginalized and oppressed people embody resurrection in our midst? Are we able to see how gay, lesbian, bisexual, and transgendered people are actually God's hope for the new community? Are we able to re-imagine those who are most oppressed, and even condemned, to be the locus of God's resurrection power? If we really want to understand the full reality of the Body of the Risen Christ, then as responsible preachers we must look for the presence of the Risen Christ in places we do not live our lives, places we would least expect, and in the lives of people we have even condemned as unworthy of blessing and resurrection life. Can we as preachers preach in such a way as to restore people's hope in the church as the Body of the Risen Christ? Have we courage enough to enable the people of God to see resurrection in places they can scarcely imagine?

2. The Resurrection as Process, Not Moment

The Brazilian theologian Leonardo Boff invites us to consider that resurrection is not always that which happens in a dramatic moment, or that which happens suddenly. Resurrection can also be a process:

> Wherever, in mortal life, goodness triumphs over the instincts of hatred, wherever one heart opens to another, wherever a righteous attitude is built and room is created for God, there the Resurrection has begun.[4]

Boff's words are powerfully true. We all know the work, the capacity, the courage, the pain out of which resurrection life emerges. Instincts of hatred are locations of death, and they are unbelievably difficult to overcome. It takes a lifetime to nurture a heart that truly has the capacity to be open and changed by another. Righteous attitudes and truths one can stake one's life upon are possible to find but rare. And creating room for God often means some form of relinquishment and single-mindedness. The truth of Boff's words reminds us why resurrection life is simultaneously wonderful and painful.

We are instructed by Boff's words, but perhaps the real hope lies in the affirmation that when these things happen in mortal life, there the resurrection has begun. Resurrection is a process, a turning, a striving, a stirring. It has as much to do with *how* we are moving through this world as *where* we end up.

The ethicist Sharon Welch joins her voice to Boff's when she affirms the power and importance of each action that is taken toward life, not just the dramatic actions that seem to bring about immediate change:

> The extent to which an action is an appropriate response to the needs of others is constituted as much by the possibilities it creates as by its immediate results.... Responsible action provides partial resolutions and the inspiration and conditions for further partial resolutions by others.[5]

Striving to overcome instincts of hatred with goodness, opening hearts to another, and the building of righteous attitudes do not always bring about immediate new life or resurrected transformation. Yet, those responsible actions help create the possibilities for countless future actions, and all of those together are powerful enough to lead to resurrection.

Gay and lesbian theologians would echo the words of Boff, for they know in a very distinct way that resurrection is not a once and for all act, but a lifetime process. They know this through the painful and liberatory actions associated with coming out. Coming out is that process of revealing the fullness of who one is as a gay or lesbian person to one's family, friends, church, employer. It is the act of making one's identity as gay or lesbian public. "Coming out in heterosexist patriarchy is a lifetime project. We need lots of time and space to feel, and become aware of, the radical significance of living as openly gay and lesbian people."[6]

For many people, and many communities, resurrection will be experienced more as a gradual process of emerging new life than as a definitive moment. It may feel more like a movement with no distinct destination ever realized. Yet all those separate moments and movements, when life is clung to, injustice denounced, and space made available and ready for future new life, participate in resurrection life.

For Easter Sunday in *Imaging the Word: An Arts and Lectionary Resource*, Volume 1, there is a piece of art entitled "Resurrection." Here is the description of that sculpture:

> Art representing the crucifixion and the risen Christ is commonly seen, but art which attempts to present the moment of resurrection is rare. In a smaller-than-life representation, Paul Granlund has attempted to interpret that moment. The figure of Christ is shown bent over, knees and head nearly touching. The arms are outstretched in a position of crucifixion. The figure is bound on three sides by slabs of the tomb and on the fourth by the earth. Close examination reveals holes in the top and in the right side-panel where the arms would have protruded when the panels were tightly closed around the body.
>
> The movement of the body is not downward, but upward and out. The outstretching of the arms and the propelling tension in the legs emphasize the surging strength of this Christ as the lid of the tomb is thrown off. The walls of death are not strong enough to prevail against the power of God. Almost birdlike, this figure is breaking free of earth's gravity, no longer under the sway of ordinary time and space. This is the power of resurrection.[7]

Can we as preachers nurture this kind of keen homiletical lens to adequately describe and proclaim the moments, movements, and processes of resurrection no matter how subtle, small, lengthy, or gradual?

3. Resurrection as Neighborhood/Community Transformation

Just as the Body of the Risen Christ describes a powerful communal image of resurrection, so does the transformation of neighborhood and community. Resurrection does not just happen to isolated individuals; it happens to entire communities of people. It is surely what happened to the early followers of Jesus on the other side of his death and resurrection as they moved from places of fear and silence into a body of resurrected power and mission.

Feminist scholars in the past two decades have been shifting christological discussions from a sole focus on Jesus as the Christ to the community as the locus of redemptive, salvific activity; from individual images of salvation to more communal ones.[8] This is a welcome corrective to christological discussions that would relegate salvific activity to individual acts. This same kind of theological work needs to be done in relation to the specific activity of resurrection. Because the Christian church continues to exist in the United States and Canada in the midst of alienating and disempowering individualism, preachers need to name and proclaim more collective images of resurrection that renew our hope in community, and hold us accountable, one to the other.

In 1993 I visited a Roman Catholic parish in downtown Los Angeles. The priest told a group of practical theologians from around the country about a group of Hispanic mothers who live in this poor and violent neighborhood. For months and years they had watched their children being shot down, murdered in front of their own homes. They decided it was time to turn their neighborhood around. They moved their bodies with steady power into places that could make a difference. They decided to raise up new life in the midst of death.

They organized together and began to face the drug dealers, the racist police, and the gang leaders who were killing their sons and daughters. They came onto the streets in groups of two and three when drug deals were taking place, and they stood, and stood, and stood, until drug deals did not happen there any longer. They marched to the police station and asked the police over and over again why they were killing their children. They organized barbecues and invited gang leaders to come and talk. Over time, the fidelity of those women transformed the entire neighborhood.[9] Perhaps resurrection has everything to do with placing our bodies someplace concretely and strategizing carefully and passionately about the kind of transformations and new life we desire and know are needed. We do not infuse places of death with resurrection life alone, nor do we raise up whole neighborhoods without significant personal risk.

Melanie May says,

> I see signs of Christ's risen body—what I name new ecclesial realties—all around the world. Among these signs, these realities, are

base communities throughout Latin America and in the Philippines, African independent churches, house churches or small groups in the United States, women's communities throughout Asia, Women-Church communities among Protestant as well as Roman Catholic women across the United States, etc. Christ is risen, indeed![10]

Women from within a parish organizing together to stop the violence in their own neighborhood is not only a new ecclesial reality, but a profound witness to the eternal hope of resurrection. They decided to be more than an "ecclesiastical institution"; rather, they decided to be the presence of the Risen Christ.

Another image of resurrection as neighborhood and community transformation comes from Central America. In 1993 two of us from United Theological Seminary of the Twin Cities went to a Roman Catholic parish in the heart of Managua, Nicaragua, for morning worship. It was Pentecost Sunday and also Mother's Day. We went there to hear the music of Flavio Galo, a well known singer who had been a part of the creation of the Nicaraguan Peasant Mass. The mass has now been banned by the church hierarchy.

We entered the church, took our seats, and waited with great antici-pation. Church was to begin at 9:00 a.m. At 9:15 the priest was not present, and the musicians decided to play celebrative music honoring the mothers who were present. The music was joyous and full of life. It was not explicitly political. After about ten minutes the priest arrived, walked down the center aisle of this small church, and began speaking to the musician we had come to hear. Soon it was clear, this was not a conversation, this was a severe chastisement. The priest said, "You have desecrated this holy space by starting the mass without me." The simple response was "We have done nothing wrong. We started the mass because you were not here, and we wanted to honor the mothers with music and song." After several angry moments, something happened I will never forget. The priest picked up the eucharistic elements, walked down the center of the church, said one last angry rebuke, got into his truck, and drove away from the church. He did not return.

In time, four or five people left; all the rest remained. The music continued. Flavio led the congregation in singing one of the songs from the Peasant Mass about the God who sweats in the street:

You are the God of the poor, the simple and human God, the God with the weather-beaten face: I have seen you in a village shop and in an inn on the road. . . . I have seen you at a lottery stall and you were not ashamed. I have seen you at the filling station testing the tires of a

truck, and even on the street patrol, in overalls and leather gloves. You
are the working God . . . the toiling Christ.[11]

After the song the mother of the Galo family, Norma, preached a
homily. Her words are the words of absolute fidelity and hope:

> If we all have been given the spirit, then we all have the right to share
> in the spirit. The holiest act is not to be bowed down, but to be
> working so the word of God has life. We must have the freedom to
> preach, and the freedom to know that God will not abandon us.
> Remember the struggle continues, we will always be here.[12]

When God's people throughout the ages have taken their stand
against injustice and oppression, and against the mighty powers of evil
that threaten to silence us and diminish our very humanness, our life is
raised and renewed. Resurrection as neighborhood and community
transformation demands that people sink down their roots and always
be there.

Can we as preachers help inspire and encourage people in our local
communities to turn their neighborhoods of alienation and violence
around? Can we preach in such a way that people will reclaim the church
from the stranglehold of affluence and privileged power and raise it up
as a place of the toiling, working God among the masses?

4. Resurrection as Bodily Integrity

Carter Heyward, in one of her many profound critiques of the church's
complicity in forming and sustaining a culture that hates the body, says:

> If we are to live with our feet on the ground, in touch with reality, we
> must help one another accept the fact that we who are christian are
> heirs to a body-despising, woman-fearing, sexually repressive religious
> tradition.[13]

In the face of a church that still values the spiritual realities of life over
the material, bodily realties of existence, and a religious tradition that
continues to dichotomize mind and body, intellect and emotions, it
would be hard to deny the role the Christian church has played in alienating human beings from their embodied existence. In the face of such
alienation, surely resurrection is profoundly connected to bodily
wholeness and integrity. By bodily integrity I am pointing to the
integration of our embodied existence; an integration that knows that
human beings are bodies, not just those who reside in bodies; an
integration that knows our bodies are finite, limited, and sacred; an
integration that believes that no particular body reflects what it means

to be human, normal, natural; an integration that knows that mind, emotions, spirit, and body coexist together in human beings and cannot be fundamentally separated; an integration that affirms that all human bodies reflect the image of God.

Melanie May, in her book about the body and resurrection, invites us into the world she has known and lived through her body. It is a world of death and resurrection. For May, the experiences of her bodily existence—being diagnosed with breast cancer, experiencing a near-death moment in the hospital years ago, being diagnosed with manic depression, and dealing with the forces of death around coming out as a lesbian woman in the church—all these experiences have led her to a very distinct embodied perspective on resurrection.[14]

She describes the time in her life when, after years of suffering from severe depression, she was finally diagnosed as bi-polar.

> At last I was relieved. I am relieved. . . . Amid all the grieving, the raging, and the relief, this diagnosis—this naming—has been a purifying fire . . . The burden of my sense of moral culpability has burned away, along with the acidity of society's judgment.[15]

She then goes on to describe the dramatic changes that have been occurring in her life on the other side of the diagnosis and on the other side of casting off lifelong feelings of inadequacy, fear, and failure:

> When I speak of presence I speak, first and foremost, of presence in my body. I live, and think, in my body, no longer alienated or abstracted as I have been most of my life. I delight in my body's desires—sensory and sexual. I savor the pleasure of aromas and beauty, of taste and touch. I honor what my body knows. More particularly, I live, and think, in my female body. I have come out as a woman! I come out convinced that what matters, for men as well as women, in the face of society's stultifying code of conformity is for each one to affirm our own uniqueness and our finitude, so we are able to respect and risk being changed by the reality of otherness.[16]

In the face of a body-alienating and body-despising culture and religious tradition, coming to be present in one's own body after years of being absent from one's own body surely is a resurrection experience. This being present in one's own body in a way that is profoundly self accepting and self affirming is at the heart of what Nancy Eiesland writes about in her book, *The Disabled God*. In the opening pages of her book she says:

> Living with a disability is difficult. Acknowledging this difficulty is not a defeat, I have learned, but a hard-won accomplishment in

learning to live a life that is not disabled. The difficulty for people with disabilities has two parts really—living our ordinary, but difficult lives, and changing structures, beliefs, and attitudes that prevent us from living ordinarily.[17]

Eiesland believes that in the face of the Christian church's historical affirmations that people with disabilities are either "divinely damned or divinely blessed,"[18] and in the face of the perception in Western culture "that disability is a private physical and emotional tragedy to be managed by psychological adjustment, rather than a stigmatized social condition to be redressed through attitudinal changes and social commitment,"[19] people with disabilities are not allowed or empowered to live "ordinary lives in unconventional bodies."[20]

The bodies and lives of people with disabilities have been "managed" rather than empowered; controlled, rather than enabled; violated and despised, rather than blessed. In so many ways, death, violence, and denial have been so all pervasive that resurrection may be more the simple, yet utterly profound opportunity to live fully and completely in one's created body for the first time. Eiesland would join May in affirming how dramatic and life changing it is to actually be present *in* one's body. She says:

> Resurrection is not about the negation or erasure of our disabled bodies in hopes of perfect images, untouched by physical disability; rather Christ's resurrection offers hope that our unconventional, and sometimes difficult bodies participate fully in the imago Dei and that God whose nature is love and who is on the side of justice and solidarity is touched by our experience.[21]

Resurrection is not a new body, nor is it some perfect body by humanly created social standards; rather, resurrection for Eiesland is the transforming experience of knowing one's disabled body is made in the image of God. This theological affirmation and the resurrection experience that flows from it are utterly dependent on the Christian church's reconstructing its theology of God and its theology of human interdependence.

In recent years Christian preachers have been asked to image God as female, Asian, African American, poor. We are now being asked to think about God as limited, disabled, changed by the experience of being incarnate in a disabled body. If God is not imaged as disabled, then how will those who are disabled ever be able to believe the resurrecting affirmation of their own beings participating in that image? When a disabled person truly knows and believes that her or his embodied whole being is made in the image of God, it must be an experience of resurrection.

In addition to the Christian church needing to change its theology of God, it also needs a deepened and changed theology of interdependence. Kathy Black, in her book, *A Healing Homiletic*, says: "A theology of interdependence honors the value of all individuals, not by what they do, but by who they are, recognizing that each and every person contributes to the community by being, not by doing."[22] The Christian church is a long way from this resurrecting affirmation. Yet, I do believe that when people who need physical assistance are seen and experienced as no less human and sacred than those who do not, and genuine reciprocity and interdependence are honored and experienced by all, it must feel like resurrection not just for someone who is disabled, but also for temporarily able-bodied people who spend their lifetimes denying and demonizing natural bodily limitations.

All human beings need bodily integration, bodily wholeness, and bodily integrity.

❖   When a woman suffering from anorexia believes and knows her body is acceptable and sacred and can eat again in a healthy manner, it must feel like resurrection.

❖   When a man who is blind knows that he does not have to be physically healed to be whole, it must feel like resurrection.

❖   When an older adult knows that speed, mobility, and bodily strength do not determine sacred worth, it must feel like resurrection.

❖   When the flashbacks stop, when night sweats cease, and when the bodily ravages of post-traumatic stress end, it must feel like resurrection.

What kind of sermons might we preach if we took the human body seriously as a locus of resurrection possibility and power? What would have to change for us to more powerfully proclaim the resurrecting message that all bodies and all people participate fully in the Imago Dei?

5. Resurrection as a Refusal to Play Cards with the Jailer

Mitsuye Yamada is a woman who was born in Japan and raised in Seattle, Washington, until the beginning of World War II when her family was removed to a concentration camp in Idaho.[23] Out of that ethnic and cultural violence, this poem arises:

Playing Cards with the Jailer
A brief metallic sound
jars
the quiet night air
hangs
in my ears.

I am playing cards with the jailer
who shifts his ample body in his chair
while I fix my smile on his cards
waiting

My eyes unfocused on the floor
behind him where a set of keys spiderlike
begins to creep slowly across the room
come on come on your play I say
To distract him I tap the table
Wait.

With a wide gesture
he picks up the keys
hangs them back on the hook
Yawns.

The inmates will keep trying will keep trying
Their collective minds pull the keys
only halfway across the room each time
The world comes awake in the morning to a stupor
My brown callused hands guard two queens and an ace
My polished pink nails shine in the almost light
I have been playing cards with jailers
for too many years.[24]

Japanese Americans who had to "play cards with the jailers" of white America during the Second World War know what it is like to be at the mercy of the powerful for their daily existence. Conversely, these same Japanese Americans must feel like they are rising up as resurrected people as they not only refuse to beg for freedom and dignity at the hands of white Euro-Americans, but as they also have organized to demand concrete material reparation for violence done, property and resources lost, and cultural degradation endured.[25]

The resurrection has been defined and proclaimed for too long by many of us who are the jailers of power and control, the jailers of privilege and imperialism. Those who have been playing cards with jailers for too many years will give us vastly different images and understandings of resurrection life and hope. What happens when someone who has been playing cards with a jailer of power and privilege lays down the cards, walks away from the table, and refuses to play?

There is a powerful testimony to the resurrection that can be found on the other side of freeing one's self from certain jailers in this life. In this case the jailer is the Christian church:

> For the past few years, resurrection has revived my life only when I have stepped away from the Presbyterian church. As a woman, a feminist, and as a lesbian, the possibility of spiritual annihilation has become too real. Death surrounds and informs much of my dealings in the Presbyterian church. The conservative activists and the silent, sleeping bulk of the church which allow them to continue unchecked in their rampage of intimidation have left my body/spirit involuntarily entombed. I have followed Jesus' call to stumble out of this tomb like Lazarus, but the church continues to keep me and my sisters and brothers firmly immobilized.
>
> For me, the Presbyterian church has become a place of continual crucifixion. . . I choose life. I choose to leave the Presbyterian church.[26]

There is a growing number of gay, lesbian, bisexual, and transgendered Christians who are prophetically indicting the church for its condemnation and its abandonment. There are also thousands and thousands of these same Christian women and men who simply have left the church because the continual crucifixions were more than they could bear. They have sought life in a multitude of other places. It is a strange and terrible irony that thousands of Christian people feel they must consciously leave the church in order to find life and God's resurrection power.

Perhaps there has never been a stronger preaching voice in exposing the kinds of death that come with "playing cards with the jailer," than Martin Luther King, Jr. This exposure happened throughout his speaking and preaching ministry, yet one moment stands out. It was April 16, 1963, during the time he was serving one of many jail sentences, that he crafted the famous "Letter from Birmingham City Jail." He wrote this letter to a group of clergy who had criticized his civil rights activity as unwise and untimely:

We know through painful experience that freedom is never voluntarily given by the oppressor; it must be demanded by the oppressed. . . . For years now I have heard the words "Wait!" It rings in the ear of every Negro with a piercing familiarity. This "Wait" has almost always meant "Never." . . . I guess it is easy for those who have never felt the stinging darts of segregation to say, "Wait." But when you have seen vicious mobs lynch your mothers and fathers at will and drown your sisters and brothers at whim; when you have seen hate-filled policemen curse, kick, brutalize, and even kill your black brothers and sisters with impunity; when you see the vast majority of your twenty million Negro brothers smothering in an airtight cage of poverty in the midst of an affluent society; when you suddenly find your tongue twisted and your speech stammering as you seek to explain to your six-year-old daughter why she can't go to the public amusement park that has just been advertised on television . . . when you are forever fighting a degenerating sense of "nobodiness"; then you will understand why we find it difficult to wait. There comes a time when the cup of endurance runs over, and men [sic] are no longer willing to be plunged into an abyss of injustice. . . . I hope, sirs, you can understand our legitimate and unavoidable impatience.[27]

It must feel like resurrection when one refuses to wait for one's human rights, when one refuses to quietly tolerate daily humiliations, and when one allows one's cup of endurance to run over into acts of resistance.

Will our preaching ministries proclaim a subtle and blatant Wait, or will our words, our visions, our truth telling enable people to tolerate the cup of endurance no longer? As terrifying as it sometimes feels to those who have power, oppressed and violated people must stop playing cards with the jailer if they are ever to know the power and possibility of resurrection in this life.

6. Resurrection as Resistance and Insurrection

Contemporary theologians and people of faith speak about resurrection and its relationship to resistance in a variety of ways:

❖ "Resurrection is radical courage."[28] When human beings face the possibilities of death on behalf of justice and the alleviation of oppressive suffering, this remarkable courage arises from God's resurrection power.

❖ "The resurrection is the final sense of insurrection for right and justice."[29] Jesus' resurrection was a proclamation to the world that insurrection against all that is unjust and all that produces death and destruction will produce the kind of holy life that can burst forth from any and all graves. Not only is

Jesus' resurrection the final sense of insurrection for justice, our resurrection experiences also are inseparably bound to the struggle for justice.

❖   "But despite the betrayal of the revolution and, God knows, the betrayal of Christ, we see happening again and again what we all need most: uprisings of life against the many forms of death; which is to say, resurrection."[30] Jesus' resurrection is God's eternal act of resistance. God's insurrection against human injustice is also expressed and embodied in every human being who refuses to abandon life, no matter what the cost.

Near the end of the month of June each year, gay, lesbian, bisexual, and transgendered people and their allies celebrate such an uprising of life. In many United States cities, the end of June is a time to commemorate and to celebrate one of the great insurrection moments in this community's life. Pride marches and festivals happen at this time because on June 27, 1969, there was a public rebellion and resistance in New York City that changed gay/lesbian/bisexual and transgendered people's history and lives. It was a time when oppressed people said "No," and that resistance changed history forever.

The evening of June 27, 1969, police raided a Greenwich Village bar, the Stonewall Inn. This was a gay bar that was the target of routine police harassment and brutality. On that night in 1969, instead of the patrons quietly accepting the actions of the arresting officers, they fought back. In fact, the insurrection and resistance lasted for days following this initial night. The rebellion surrounding the Stonewall Inn in 1969 is not to be romanticized. A lot of people were injured, and it was a frightening time. Yet for the gay/lesbian/bisexual and transgendered community it was an absolute experience of resurrection. There were many historical groups formed and actions taken before Stonewall that allowed this moment to be so transformative, yet few people would disagree that it stands out as utterly distinct in the community's history. Martin Duberman describes Stonewall with these words:

> "Stonewall" is the emblematic event in modern lesbian and gay history. . . . "Stonewall" has become synonymous over the years with gay resistance to oppression. . . . The 1969 riots are now generally taken to mark the birth of the modern gay and lesbian political movement — that moment in time where gays and lesbians recognized all at once their mistreatment and their solidarity. As such, "Stonewall" has become an empowering symbol of global proportions.[31]

There was an uprising of life at Stonewall, and there was a moment when courageous people took to the streets with a loud insurrection/ resurrection "No!"

Insurrection/resistance moments in life are filled with holy paradox. Almost always the risks are very high, and the costs can be horrific. Yet, simultaneously, moments when people are resisting abuse, oppression, and violence and are refusing the threat of death itself are moments when resurrection life, new life, is born.

The Montgomery Bus Boycott of the mid-1950s, and the specific resistance of Rosa Parks and her refusal to relinquish her seat to a white man, were moments of resistance and insurrection that turned the course of history in the Civil Rights Movement in this country. Acts of civil disobedience and intervention by members of Greenpeace have actually saved the lives of endangered species and humanized us all in our relationship with creation. Women and men and children protesting at missile sites and nuclear waste dumps have been able, at times, to radically change public policy. These are moments of resistance and insurrection that lead from death to life, from destruction to preservation, from dehumanization to dignity. This is God's resurrecting activity.

And let us not be tempted to think acts of resistance and insurrection are insignificant or unimportant within the massive, systemic structure of our day for these acts do make a radical difference. There is a dedication page in the book *The Montgomery Bus Boycott and the Women Who Started It: The Memoir of JoAnn Gibson Robinson* that describes the impact of the boycott on her own life and the lives of many others:

> Boycotting taught me courage. The memory of the thousands of boycotters, walking in hot and cold weather, in rain, sleet, and sunshine, for thirteen long months, makes me feel ever so humble. These people inspired me to refuse to accept what was wrongfully imposed upon me. Justice in the end was the coveted goal that helped and inspired me and fifty thousand others to become involved. Their suffering cannot be adequately told. These are the people who sacrificed. The people did it![32]

Sometimes the impact of an individual and/or communal act of resistance can lead to fifty thousand people staging a boycott against injustice and violence. These acts give rise to courage and to persevering life. They also have the power to shape and form a group of individuals into an organized collective force for change. There is a powerful link between courage, renewed dignity, and resurrection.

Do we, in our preaching ministries, preach a gospel of resistance and insurrection, or a gospel of accommodation and passive acceptance? Do we encourage people to embody radical courage even if it leads them to acts of insurrection against the powers of government or church? What would it look like, sound like, and feel like to preach Jesus' resurrection as God's eternal act of resistance and insurrection?

7. Resurrection as Coming Out

Heterosexism is one of the fundamental structures of our social reality. It is built upon the assumption that relationships between females and males have primary relational meaning, exclusive social sanction, and superior moral and ethical value. Lesbians and gay men are not simply made invisible in the social fabric of our nations and in the community life of most of our churches; they are actively excluded, harassed, and persecuted. The relational and social values and experiences of gay men and lesbians are not simply silenced; they are judged inferior, deviant, and sick. In the face of persistent bodily, economic, spiritual, and ecclesiastical silence and violence, coming out has everything to do with resistance and new life. In the face of statistics that tell us that teenagers who are struggling with issues of sexual orientation are three times more likely to commit suicide than their peers,[33] coming out has everything to do with resurrection.

In the play, *Coming Out, Coming Home*, a young, closeted gay man gives us a picture, a taste, a feeling, of what the process of resurrection feels like:

> It was three nights before I mustered the courage to venture out. I borrowed my father's car and drove downtown. It was winter, cold and windy, but even so I parked some five blocks away from the bar. God forbid the car shouldn't start, and I'd have to explain getting it jumped near a gay bar.
>
> I braced myself and opened the door. A blast of warm air greeted me and my glasses fogged over at once. As I pulled my glasses off to clean them, I heard the sound of music in the background.
>
> As I looked across that room I realized I knew something intimate about each and every one there. And just by my being there, they knew something about me. That thing that I had hidden, and run from, and denied. We shared our secrets en masse, silently amidst the blaring music.
>
> I felt as though I'd come home. Like I'd found a long lost family or tribe. I felt affirmed and good about myself. It wouldn't have had to have been a bar. It could have been anywhere. Anywhere that gay people were gathered together, happy, and at peace. It could have even been in a church. But it wasn't.[34]

Many gay and lesbian people are looking for a sense of home that will break into the profound isolation they experience on a daily basis. When they find it with other gay and lesbian people, often it feels like a kind of resurrection.

Lesbians and gay men describe this resurrection experience in a variety of ways:

❖   "No matter how much the church has conditionalized God's love for gay and lesbian Christians, God's 'Yes in Christ' graciously bursts forth, wrapping divine arms around us, welcoming us home."[35] Somehow even though the church has often been the vehicle of condemnation, God as witnessed in the life and ministry of Jesus the Christ still reaches and surrounds gay and lesbian people with a death-defeating grace and love.

❖   "After all the fear, lying, and hiding, telling the truth is positively sacramental. It is a rite of purification."[36] Authenticity and an integrated sense of one's identity are critical dimensions in human health and well-being. Coming out has the sacramental possibility of enabling lesbians and gay men to cast off guilt, shame, and self-loathing. This purging, this purifying, this casting off, is surely the salvific activity of resurrection life.

❖   "The phrase *coming out* is of course metaphorical. . . . The metaphor suggests a contrast between stasis and movement, stasis with its apparent safety, security, protection (because we remain a member of the dominant heterosexual group); movement which means an engaging of the self and others through action and the taking of risks. . . . Like the nautilus, each of us must risk vacating chamber after chamber as it grows too confining for her emerging self, in order to create her own new, larger space."[37]

In addition to these images of resurrection, it is no happenstance that many gay and lesbian people associate the new life of baptism with the whole process of coming out: "In a Christian context, coming-out rituals may incorporate symbols and language from baptismal renewal rites. . . . The ritual proclaims by word and symbol that this person has journeyed out of silence and death into new life and a new community."[38] Not only does coming out join one to whole dimensions of one's self that have been denied, forgotten, or repressed, but coming out resurrects gay and lesbian people into a new community that will be the community which often will sustain their very lives.

Coming out involves countless acts of courage and risk. Coming out involves acts of rising out of graves of silence and death and vacating chambers of comfort, familiarity, and safety. Coming out is a movement toward coming home to one's self, one's community, one's people. Carter Heyward would say it is a way of coming into our "Yes."[39]

If coming out can be a resurrection experience for so many gay and lesbian people and the church demands secrecy, silence, and closets, then as a student in one of my classes once said, "The church has abandoned sites of resurrection."[40]

Do the words and messages of our sermons keep people in alienating closets of lies and secrets, or do our sermons help open those suffocating doors? What would it look like and sound like if preachers of the Christian church were to claim the sites of coming out as sites of resurrection and places and moments of God's salvific activity?

8. Resurrection as Remembrance and Presence

In 1988 I went to see the Names Project Quilt in Washington, D.C. It is a living, growing memorial to the thousands of people who have died from AIDS. At 7:10 a.m. the quilt began to be unfolded, and from then until 6:00 in the evening, names were read: "Mike Belt, Michael Collins, Lynn Carter, Leroy Estrada, Katie Mitchell, Lee, Stephen, Tom, my brother, those without a hand to hold."

As you walk around the quilt you see lovers weeping, running their fingers over the names of those they have loved. You see families standing in silence. You overhear friends telling stories. You see thousands of others looking, searching for names, searching for a tangible sign that death has not had the final word. All who make this quilt, all who work to display it, all who come to see it, are looking for redemption in the midst of this modern-day crucifixion.

When viewing this quilt, one is never unaware of the horrible suffering and death that accompanies AIDS; it is the power of love and life that prevails in the presence of this gigantic public memorial and tribute. It is a loud resounding "No" to death, "No" to forgetting, "No" to shame, "No" to isolation, and "No" to denial. In each "No," there is a simultaneous "Yes" to life.

Sweet Honey In The Rock sing their own distinctive tribute to both the quilt and the lives it represents.

Patchwork Quilt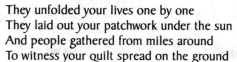

They unfolded your lives one by one
They laid out your patchwork under the sun
And people gathered from miles around
To witness your quilt spread on the ground

Refrain:
  And then they called out your name
  And then they called out your name
  O and you will live forever
  You know that I'll be loving you just like a patchwork quilt

Well there were men and women, mothers and fathers.
Sisters and brother, daughters and sons
And children and babies, and lovers and friends
They all lay before me sewn into one

Your lives had meaning, your lives had joy
You touched so many people, many more than you will know
And you wrapped yourselves around me
As I walked down these rows
You're letting me feel your beautiful souls

Refrain:
  I feel the warmth of your lives
  I feel the warmth of your lives
  You know that I'll be loving you just like a patchwork quilt

My heart spills over, flowing with tears
I cry for your suffering and for your shortened years
And I'll take you with me as I walk away
Remembering you who have died with AIDS

Refrain:
  Yes, I remember your names
  Yes, I remember your names
  You know that I'll be loving you
  Just like a patchwork quilt
  I'll be loving you like a patchwork quilt[41]

The flyers that accompany this extraordinary quilt say: "Turn the power of the quilt into action!" This quilt is not just about personal remembering, although that is powerful and holy in its own right. The making and displaying of this quilt are acts of remembrance that keep fueling whole communities and organizations in their work to find a cure for AIDS, in their work to provide dignified hospice care, in their work to secure affordable medication and equitable health care. It is a quilt that fuels resistance with the living presence of all those who have died.

Sharon Welch has taken memory and the act of remembering as serious focal points for theology throughout her work. In describing the discipline and practice of liberation theology, she describes "dangerous memory" that has two dimensions: one of remembering suffering and one of recounting hope.[42]

Liberation theology understands with absolute clarity the essential importance of human remembering. Human beings who suffer oppression must never be forgotten: those who have suffered from oppression and violence in the past, and those who continue to suffer in the present. Not only must the suffering be remembered, but the human agency of all those who have struggled to resist their own and others' oppression must be remembered as well. We remember so that someday we might not continue to repeat the horrible atrocities that seem to persist. "Memories of struggle against social systems are dangerous; they are witnesses to protests against an order of things that claims to be natural, self-evident, or inevitable,"[43] which Welch describes as "memory as critique."[44]

But there must not only be memory as critique and the remembering of suffering. There must also be the act of remembering hope, the memory of freedom and resistance.[45] We remember to keep alive the resistance struggles of those who have gone before us so they can fuel our own. The AIDS quilt serves to spark both memory as critique and memory as hope and resistance, and both are needed if remembering is to become an act of resurrection or a practice that refuses to abandon life.

Latin American people of faith and the theologians that arise from Central and South America keep before us images of dangerous memory as well. One of the most poignant surrounds the living memory and presence of Oscar Romero of El Salvador. Oscar Romero was an archbishop of El Salvador who became an outspoken voice against oppression and in practice in his country, even though the institution of the church threatened to silence him. Jon Sobrino asks the question: "Where Is Archbishop Romero Alive Today?":

> In order to answer this first question, we need only allow our gaze to wander over the multitudes of the Salvadoran people. In their shelters, in the base communities of poor believers, in the parishes, in the religious communities of those who work with all of these other communities, a portrait, a poster—or, among the very poorest, a faded photograph clipped from a newspaper—of Archbishop Romero is always there. In their liturgical celebrations, in the meetings in which they decide what to do, and what to say to God, what difficulties to try to overcome and what commitments to take up, where to find the strength for forgiveness and reconciliation—the memory of Archbishop Romero is always fresh and alive. . . . Archbishop Romero lives where he has always lived: in the poor of his people.
>
> The life of Archbishop Romero today is like that of Jesus. It is a resurrected life. Archbishop Romero is *risen from the dead*. That is, he lives by pouring his spirit into the Salvadoran people.[46]

It is not just that Romero is remembered as someone from the past; rather, he accompanies the people in the present. He is present when they make decisions, when they worship, when they struggle to forgive, and when they work for peace, justice, and reconciliation. Bodily death cannot silence or defeat the vitality and witness of his life. Romero himself understood this image of resurrection keenly. Even before he died he spoke about how he would rise again in the people of El Salvador. Just a few days before he was murdered he said these words:

> I must tell you, as a Christian, I do not believe in death without resurrection. If I am killed, I shall arise in the Salvadoran people. . . . If the threats are carried out, from this moment I offer my blood to God for the redemption and for the resurrection of El Salvador.[47]

Resurrection as remembrance, as subversive memory, as dangerous memory, as living presence, as seed for new life, and as corrective and direction: All are powerful, redemptive images. The act of remembering resurrects people, creates energy, vision, and life to change the present and helps us live differently in the future.

One of the most memorable photographs that has been taken at The Wall, the Vietnam War Memorial in Washington D.C., shows a veteran looking at the wall holding a very large sign that reads: "I am a Vietnam veteran. I like the memorial. And if it makes it difficult to send people into battle again . . . I'll like it even more."[48] May our experiences of remembrance and presence not only make it more difficult to participate in the forces of death that surround us, but also may they help us all subversively and dangerously refuse to abandon life.

How will our preaching participate in this subversive, dangerous memory? What will we choose to make present in our sermons so that it becomes more difficult for people to participate in death? What walls of remembrance will we create with our words, our stories, our images, and our passion, so that the next time it might be different?

9. Practicing Resurrection

Returning to Melanie May, we read: "I *practice* resurrection . . . Amid the mysterious and often tragic mingling of grief and ecstasy, dying and rising . . . I practice but I do not celebrate resurrection."[49] May honors both the truth of our lives and the truth and complexity of resurrection with her honest words. Resurrection is an experience inseparably linked with death. Being the Body of the Risen Christ can raise a people up into new life, and it can also bring death into the same people's lives. Coming out can be a burst of authentic life, and it can also bring abandonment and condemnation. Resurrection can fuel insurrection, and the repression that follows can be swift and bloody.

However, we are called to proclaim resurrection even in the midst of death, even in the midst of struggle, even in the midst of terror. All the images, stories, poetry, and quotes previously shared attest to that truth. We practice resurrection in the midst of death. We live it in the midst of death. We celebrate it in the midst of death.

There is a powerful global image of resurrection as practice. It is an image that has become known throughout the world. It is the image of The Mothers of the Plaza de Mayo in Buenos Aires, Argentina.

For over twenty years, fifty to seventy mothers have come to the plaza bearing witness to the absence of their disappeared loved ones. In the face of many differences, a missing child brought them all together. At least thirty thousand children have disappeared in Argentina, and often they were children who raised questions about justice, who were not afraid to confront authority. In the beginning only a handful of women came, but gradually the numbers grew. The mothers gather at a central plaza, wearing white kerchiefs on their heads and carrying pictures of their children. At 3:30 every Thursday afternoon, they march around the plaza. They march in the face of no answers about their children's disappearances. They march knowing their children are probably dead. They march in the face of more children made to disappear.

They march in the face of mothers disappearing. They march in the face of endless violence.[50]

These Mothers of the Plaza de Mayo have been practicing resurrection for over two decades. Their practicing and their great moments of celebration and hope can be heard around the globe. One of the founding mothers writes these words:

> Yes, each of us Mothers is born again in the circle ... every Thursday we are a dispersed army which regroups at three-thirty in the afternoon. One Mother leaves her apron in the kitchen, another her sewing machine, yet another her typewriter.... What mysterious hand convoked us? The puzzle of our children's fate, which didn't stop us from going on ... the son's photograph on the night table; every Thursday it would point the way—"Today is the circle, Mom—to the Plaza!"[51]
>
> The Mother's circle still goes on.... We continue to go to the Plaza in order to keep alive the fire we lit on the first day.[52]

It is in the practicing of resurrection that the mothers keep that fire alive. It is in the practicing of resurrection that the mothers keep their children alive. It is in the practicing of resurrection that the mothers keep a vision of hope and justice alive for themselves, their country, and the world. The resurrection practices of these mothers have sparked and raised up similar protests for human rights and similar movements of mothers in countless other countries.

Will our preaching ministries inspire people to practice resurrection in the midst of situations that seem without social and political hope? Will our preaching encourage people to form collective marches against injustices even when the forces of death seem to absolutely prevail?

Proclaiming Resurrection Anew

We have explored many complex and challenging images of resurrection: resurrection as the Risen Body of Christ and God's hope for the new community; resurrection as process, not moment; resurrection as neighborhood and community transformation; resurrection as bodily integrity; resurrection as a refusal to play cards with the jailer; resurrection as resistance and insurrection; resurrection as coming out; resurrection as remembrance and presence; and resurrection as that which we practice. May these images challenge and inspire us in our proclamations of God's word. May these images lead us to claim and name every conceivable expression of resurrection life among us. May we as preachers re-image resurrection boldly, and may we, and those we share life and ministry with, practice it faithfully and persistently.

RESURRECTION—CROSSING OVER BODIES

Read Matthew 16: 21–26

Deny yourself . . . take up your cross . . . lose your life . . .
At a time when the Christian church is beginning to see the destructive impact of its theology on the real lives of people, these words seem strange and downright offensive. There is a part of me that wants to rage against these ancient words, for far too many people's lives have already been denied. Crucifixions still abound, and the lost lives of humanity haunt us daily. I am ready to say a loud "No!" No more self denial, no more crosses, no more lost lives.

"From that time on, Jesus began to show his disciples that he must go to Jerusalem and undergo great suffering at the hands of the elders and chief priests and scribes, and be killed, and on the third day be raised."

Going to Jerusalem—if it is only a movement toward a predestined crucifixion that we continue to celebrate, then I would not want to be standing among you. I can no longer celebrate any kind of crucifixion, and I do not see Jesus as a passive sacrifice. If taking up crosses, denying self, and losing one's life only serve to justify the horrors of human suffering among us, then I would want to join the Hebrew Bible scholar, Phyllis Trible, in suggesting that this is a "Text of Terror" rather than the good news of the gospel.

"Deny yourself . . . take up your cross . . . and follow."

In reality, there is a part of me that wants to scream across these miles and years, "Go back, Jesus. Run for your life while you still can. Try some different strategy. Hide for a while." Yet in the midst of this temptation, I know that the words of songwriter Holly Near are absolutely true: "There ain't no where you can run no, no, no. There ain't no where you can run." Her words go on to say, "You can hand out flowers in airports, You can stay on your knees and pray. But there ain't no where in this whole wide world that you can run away."[53]

Holly is singing about nuclear rain but the lyrics are timeless, for we know they could be about some of the atrocities and horrors of human existence during any age and every age. This song helps me move a little deeper into the meaning of self denial, crosses, and losing one's life.

Jesus did not run. I don't understand why he did not run, but he didn't. And because of that fact, all of our lives are different. Because we know the story well, the fact that he did not run is even more poignant. We know some of what is coming. In the days that follow this prediction of his passion, betrayals are exposed, friends sit at the table together and fight, chosen disciples argue over who is the greatest, the crowds rail out in violence, and Jesus' body is finally nailed to a cross.

I identify more with Peter, with his profound "God forbid it," than I will ever identify with Jesus going headlong into the realities of human suffering and death. Perhaps Peter is simply unwilling to accept the inevitable price of radical love. Can you blame him? Maybe he is desperately hoping there will be some miraculous strategy, some alternative vision, some critical moment of decision that will keep violence and death away. I know this denial. It is the stuff of my every-day life. It does not seem all that unreasonable or unhealthy. Who of us wants to face into the worst we can imagine? Who of us chooses to travel into every painful transformation that we actually can avoid? Do we always have to grasp the raw and painful parts of life, know and understand every difficult truth, and take the veils off of every form of oppression and injustice?

Several years ago at Christmastime I opened a small package from my sister Pam. It was a framed quote by an anonymous Catholic worker. The quote read, "When they come for the innocent without crossing over your body, cursed be your religion and your life." The boldness and truth of these words make me want to weep, and they cast a strange new shadow upon denial, crosses and losing one's life. "There ain't no where you can run, no, no, no" spills over into powerful indictment and wondrous hope.

Going to Jerusalem is about crossing over bodies: Jesus' body, your body, my body. It is about being there. It is about chaining ourselves to gates, emptying bedpans, living in war zones while hanging on to life, working in the inner city, stroking foreheads, learning to sign with our hands. It is about ultimate meaning, religious commitment, passionate life.

The kind of cross Jesus speaks of does not just celebrate the absence of running. It celebrates the presence of embodied love, placing one's flesh and blood wherever the innocent are violated and oppressed, wherever people hurt and suffer, wherever people long for new life.

This is no disembodied faith. Sometimes it is dramatic and public. It is the martyr's blood that rises again in the people of El Salvador. It is the voice of children breaking the silence of parental incest. It is the mothers of the disappeared in Guatemala running their fingers through the dirt of clandestine graves in hopes of identifying the remains of loved ones. It is the incarnated presence of English and Welsh women at Gresham Peace Encampment in England who pitched their lives around the perimeter of a missile base for years—not months, but years. It is the witness of men and women in Greenpeace boats placing bodies between commercial ships and magnificent whales. And it is the protective protest of native people in this country trying to preserve sacred land. It is the witness of gay, lesbian, bisexual people linking their lives to form a church.

Sometimes embodied faith is quiet and private. It is there as lovers hold each other in hospital beds, as condoms are used intentionally and with care, as babies are nursed, as children are fed, as people find safety in each others' arms, as wounded people find within themselves the strength to forgive, as a hand is extended to a stranger.

I believe that when these things happen in our common life, whenever and wherever people refuse to abandon life, we are standing in the presence of resurrection. I have come to believe that resurrection life is not just something that comes at the end of life or at the end of struggle and death, but something that comes in the midst of it.

Joanne Brown and Rebecca Parker speak about this in an article entitled, "For God So Loved the World":

> Resurrection means that death is overcome in those precise instances when human beings choose life, refusing the threat of death. Jesus climbed out of the grace in the Garden of Gethsemane when he refused to abandon his commitment to the truth even though his enemies threatened him with death. On Good Friday, the Resurrected One was Crucified.[54]

I have come to believe that Jesus spent his whole ministry climbing out of graves of death. So many people had to cross over his body in so many places, he had to be destroyed.

When people pour out their lifeblood and lay down their bodies, even death itself is helpless to overcome the power and possibility of these moments. This is not facing into death as an end in itself or as any idealized self-sacrifice. This is a facing into death because life, justice, liberation, and protection of the innocent require it.

When people face into extreme vulnerability, their own greatest fears, the mighty powers of alienation, the stifling seduction of comfort and control, death and meaninglessness are helpless to overcome the power and possibility of these moments. Here is life that is so strong, so sure, so full, so clear, it pries open tombs, releases chains, and raises people right up out of the grave.

When Christians use the language of self-denial, crosses, and losing one's life, I want to believe that we are saying a profound "Yes" to every human being who has ever been courageous enough to face into the worst we can imagine, the hardest we can imagine, in order to shape a world that is the best we can imagine; and that we are saying "Yes" to life and "No" to death and sacrifice as ends in themselves.

Human beings who refuse to abandon life, who know what is possible and are willing to live that possibility, teach us how to do the same. When I want to be reminded of what embodied presence looks like, I watch the movie *Romero* again. Many of us in the Christian community have seen that movie in recent years and come away reeling from its violence and its hope. The movie focuses on a segment of the life and ministry of Archbishop Oscar Romero of El Salvador. He is a man who loves his people and is struggling to know how to be faithful to them and to the mandates of the gospel. In the beginning, he struggles to keep the Christian church and the political repression of his country separate. In the end, he is assassinated because he has become one of the most outspoken voices of truth and confrontation. His is a journey toward resurrection.

One of the most haunting and inspiring scenes in the movie takes place after one of the churches within his realm of responsibility has been taken over by the military, and no one is permitted to enter. The church has become a barracks. Archbishop Romero walks past the guards at the entrance to the church, down the center aisle, and up to the altar. He tells the guard that he has come to remove the host, the blessed sacrament. The guard laughs, turns, and opens machine gun fire on the entire altar area.

Romero leaves, walks outside the church, views the faces, the eyes, the silent courage of the people, then walks back inside the church. He walks up to the altar, bends down on his hands and knees, and picks up pieces of the host in his hands. All the while, the same guard fires his gun over Romero's head. Romero walks out of the church and drives away in a car, only to return moments later. He steps out of the car, puts on his alb, and then his stole, and leads the people past the guards back into their church.[55]

Putting on one's stole must be like going to Jerusalem, must be like facing into the worst we can imagine, must feel like climbing out of the grave of death.

And let us never forget that one must choose to pick up and put on a stole over and over again. One must choose to go into Jerusalem each and every time. One must spend a lifetime climbing out of graves and placing one's body nearer the innocent and oppressed.

It is painfully hard to climb out of graves, to put stoles on, to lay down our bodies. This resurrection power is created, nurtured, and sustained in community, in places where people call each other forth from death into life.

Jack Pantaleo, a gay man who writes about his recovery from being raped by a stranger, speaks vividly about the power of community in helping us climb out of the grave:

> On the anniversary of the rape, a group of my closest friends held a healing service in my apartment. They laid hands on me to pray away the degradation from that awful night. After the service, one of my friends stayed with me the entire night and held me. My community reached their hands into my tomb of self hate and doubt and loved me. They untied my grave clothes with the most unrelenting tenderness.[56]

This is what Jesus' words ultimately call us to: untying grave clothes with unrelenting tenderness, facing into all those things that keep life from being blessing for all, putting on stoles, climbing out of graves, and forcing people to step over us on their way to the innocent.

"Deny yourself . . . take up your cross . . . lose your life."

A text of terror—indeed it is!

Notes

Chapter 1: Resurrection in This Life

1. Miriam Therese Winter, *God-with-Us: Resources for Prayer and Praise* (Nashville: Abingdon, 1979), 83. Winter is quoting from Anthony Padovano's *Free To Be Faithful* (Paramus, N.J.: Paulist Press, 1972), 31.

2. Joanne Carlson Brown and Rebecca Parker, "For God So Loved the World," *Christianity, Patriarchy, and Abuse: A Feminist Critique*, ed. Joanne Carlson Brown and Carole R. Bohn (New York: The Pilgrim Press, 1989), 28.

Chapter 2: Refusing to Abandon Life

1. Henry H. Mitchell, *Black Preaching: The Recovery of a Powerful Art* (Nashville: Abingdon Press, 1990), 21.

2. Carter Heyward, *The Redemption of God: A Theology of Mutual Relation* (Washington D.C.: University Press of America, 1982), and *Touching Our Strength: The Erotic as Power and the Love of God* (San Francisco: Harper & Row, 1989). In both books Heyward sets forth aspects of her theology of mutual relation, a theological project that permeates most of her published work.

3. Leonardo Boff, *When Theology Listens to the Poor* (San Francisco: Harper & Row, 1988), 39.

4. Christine M. Smith, *Preaching as Weeping, Confession, and Resistance: Radical Responses to Radical Evil* (Louisville: Westminster/John Knox Press, 1992).

5. Rita Nakashima Brock, "And a Little Child Will Lead Us: Christology and Child Abuse," *Christianity, Patriarchy, and Abuse*, 54.

6. bell hooks [Gloria Watkins], *Teaching to Transgress: Education as the Practice of Freedom* (New York: Routledge, 1994), 74.

7. M. Shawn Copeland, "Wading through Many Sorrows," *A Troubling in My Soul: Womanist Perspectives on Evil and Suffering*, ed. Emilie M. Townes (Maryknoll, N.Y.: Orbis Books, 1993), 109–29. See these pages for a much fuller exploration of a theology of suffering from her distinct womanist perspective.

8. Mary K. DeShazer, *A Poetics of Resistance: Women Writing in El Salvador, South Africa, and the United States* (Ann Arbor: University of Michigan Press, 1994), 311. DeShazer quotes Nelson Mandela's comments on the book jacket of Carolyn Forche's book, *Against Forgetting*.

9. Eleazar S. Fernandez, *Toward a Theology of Struggle* (Maryknoll, N.Y.: Orbis Books, 1994), 23.

10. Ada María Isasi-Díaz, "Elements of a Mujerista Anthropology," *In the Embrace of God: Feminist Approaches to Theological Anthropology*, ed. Ann O'Hara Graff (Maryknoll: N.Y. Orbis Books, 1995), 91–93.

11. William Sloane Coffin, *A Passion for the Possible: A Message to U.S. Churches* (Louisville: Westminster/John Knox Press, 1993), 88.

12. DeShazer, *A Poetics of Resistance*, 271.

13. Pedro Casaldáliga and José-María Vigil, *Political Holiness: A Spirituality of Liberation* (Maryknoll, N.Y.: Orbis Books, 1994), 21–22.

14. Ibid., 22.

15. Ibid., 22–23.

16. Ibid., 23.

17. Ibid., 24.

18. Ibid.

19. Iris Marion Young, "The Five Faces of Oppression," *Justice and the Politics of Difference* (Princeton, N.J.: Princeton University Press, 1990), 40.

20. Christine Smith, *Preaching as Weeping, Confession, and Resistance*. The entire book seeks to do what is described here.

21. Louis Evely, "Fortunate Are the Poor in Spirit," *Imaging the Word: An Arts and*

Lectionary Resource, vol. 1, ed. Kenneth T. Lawrence, (Cleveland: United Church Press, 1994), 135. Used by permission.

22. Libby Roderick, "Cradle of Dawn," from the recording *If You See a Dream* (Anchorage: Turtle Island Records, 1990). Used by permission.

23. Julia Esquivel, *Threatened with Resurrection: Prayers and Poems from an Exiled Guatemalan* (Elgin: Brethren Press, 1982), 65. Used by permission.

24. Sylvia Dunstan, "Bless Now, O God, the Journey," *In Search of Hope and Grace: 40 Hymns and Gospel Songs* (Chicago: GIA Publications, 1991), 49. Used by permission.

25. Sweet Honey In The Rock, "Step By Step," from the album *The Other Side* (Chicago: Flying Fish Records, 1985). Sweet Honey has paraphrased an anonymous quote that appears in Maier Bryan Fox, *United We Stand: The United Mine Workers of America 1890–1990* (Washington, D.C.: United Mine Workers, 1990), 1.

Chapter 3: Drinking Pain and Resisting Crucifixions

1. Nancy Scheper-Hughes, *Death without Weeping: The Violence of Everyday Life in Brazil* (Berkeley: University of California Press, 1992), 128.

2. Kathy Black, *A Healing Homiletic: Preaching and Disability* (Nashville: Abingdon Press, 1996), 11.

3. John Fortunato, *Embracing the Exile: Healing Journeys of Gay Christians* (San Francisco: Harper & Row, 1982), 35.

4. Scheper-Hughes, *Death Without Weeping*, 403.

5. Boff, *When Theology Listens to the Poor*, 110–11.

6. Jon Sobrino, *Jesus the Liberator: A Historical-Theological View* (Maryknoll, N.Y.: Orbis Books, 1993), 255.

7. Marie Fortune, "Transformation of Suffering: A Biblical and Theological Perspective," *Christianity, Patriarchy, and Abuse*, 141–44.

8. Patricia Wismer, "For Women in Pain: A Feminist Theology of Suffering," *In the Embrace of God*, 142.

9. Sobrino, *Jesus the Liberator*, 262–63. Sobrino is quoting Ignácio Ellacuria.

10. Heyward, *Speaking of Christ: A Lesbian Feminist Voice* (New York: The Pilgrim Press, 1989), 13.

11. Ibid., 20.

12. Scheper-Hughes, *Death without Weeping*, 533.

13. Katie G. Cannon, *Black Womanist Ethics* (Atlanta: Scholars Press, 1988). The entire volume is a setting forth of this theological and ethical agenda.

14. Ibid. Chapters 4 and 5 explore more fully the meaning of invisible dignity, quiet grace, and unshouted courage as expressions of moral and ethical agency in the lives of black women.

15. Delores S. Williams, *Sisters in the Wilderness: The Challenge of Womanist God-Talk* (Maryknoll, N.Y.: Orbis Books, 1993), 144.

16. Ibid. This is one of the fundamental arguments that weaves its way through the entire book.

17. Ibid. Throughout the entire volume Williams builds new theological and ethical understandings and invites the reader to consider wilderness as a critical alternative to exodus as the locus of God's redemptive activity.

18. Donna Kate Rushin, "The Bridge Poem," *This Bridge Called My Back: Writings by Radical Women of Color*, ed. Cherrie Moraga and Gloria Anzaldua (New York: Kitchen Table Press, 1984), xxi–xxii.

19. Gloria Anzaldúa, *Borderlands: The New Mestiza* (San Francisco: Spinsters/Aunt Lute, 1987). Anzaldúa uses the image of borderlands to describe the lived reality of so many Chicana women who exist within both Mexican and Anglo worlds.

20. Ibid., 4.

21. Chung Hyun Kyung, *Struggle to Be the Sun Again: Introducing Asian Women's Theology* (Maryknoll, N.Y.: Orbis Books, 1990), 23.

22. Valerie Saiving, "The Human Situation: A Feminine View," *Womanspirit Rising: A Feminist Reader in Religion*, ed. Carol P. Christ and Judith Plaskow (San Francisco: Harper & Row, 1979), 25–42.

23. Susan Thistlethwaite, *Sex, Race, and God: Christian Feminism in Black and White* (New York: Crossroad, 1989), 89.

24. Ibid., 90.

25. David Buttrick, *The Mystery and the Passion: A Homiletic Reading of the Gospel Traditions* (Minneapolis: Fortress Press, 1992), 96.

26. Ibid., 101.

27. Brock, *Journeys by Heart: A Christology of Erotic Power* (New York: Crossroad, 1988), 55.

28. Carol J. Adams, "Toward a Feminist Theology of Religion and the State," *Violence against Women and Children: A Christian Theological Sourcebook*, ed. Carol J. Adams and Marie M. Fortune (New York: Continuum, 1995), 15.

29. Brock, *Journeys by Heart*. See particularly chapter 3.

30. Ibid., 69.

31. Ibid. This assertion is argued throughout the book.

32. Sobrino, *Jesus the Liberator*, 226.

33. C. S. Song, *Jesus, the Crucified People* (Minneapolis: Fortress Press, 1990), 98–99.

34. Ibid.

35. Ibid., 99.

36. See Sobrino's *Christology at the Crossroads* and Boff's *Jesus Christ Liberator* as two important examples.

37. Wismer, *In the Embrace of God*, 142.

38. Ibid., 142.

39. Brown and Parker, "For God So Loved the World," 19.

40. Song, *Jesus, the Crucified People*, 33–57.

41. Ibid., 80–99.

42. Ibid., 102–03.

43. Ibid., 103–08.

44. Ibid., 103–04.

45. Ibid. See his fuller discussion on pages 103–08.

46. Ibid., 108.

47. Ibid., 109.

48. Ibid., 110.

49. Ibid., 111.

50. Ibid. Song actually uses the term "the mute God," a term I find unhelpful and offensive in terms of issues surrounding disabilities.

51. Ibid., 112.

52. Ibid., 113.

53. Ibid., 114.

54. Ibid., 115.

55. Ibid., 116.

56. Ibid., 117.

57. Ibid., 119.

58. Ibid.

59. Ibid.

60. I recently discovered this painting in Masao Takenako and Ron O'Grady, *The Bible through Asian Eyes* (Auckland, New Zealand: Pace Publishing, 1991), 109. The artist's name is Lina Pontebon.

61. Song, *Jesus, the Crucified People*. The entire parable is told on pages 129–31. The specific words quoted here appear on page 131.

62. Ibid., 132–33.

63. Sobrino, *The Principle of Mercy: Taking the Crucified People from the Cross* (Maryknoll, N.Y.: Orbis Books), 1994.

64. Sobrino, *Jesus the Liberator*, 262–63.

65. This happened in a class at Princeton Theological Seminary in my early years of teaching. The sermon reference is from Elie Wiesel's story, "Night," found in *The Night Trilogy* (New York: The Noonday Press, 1988), 71–72.

66. Esquivel, "The Sigh," *The Certainty of Spring: Poems by a Guatemalan in Exile* (Washington, D.C.: Ecumenical Program on Central America and the Caribbean, 1993), 22. Used by permission.

67. The scene happens in the movie *Sarafina!*, dir. Darrell Roodt, 98 min. (Buena Vista Home Video, 1992, videocassette.)

Chapter 4: Risking the Terror of Resurrection

1. Robert H. Smith, *Easter Gospels: The Resurrection of Jesus According to the Four Evangelists* (Minneapolis: Augsburg, 1983), 199.

2. Ibid.

3. Xavier Leon-Dufour, *Resurrection and the Message of Easter* (New York: Holt, Rinehart and Winston, 1971), 81.

4. An example of such thinking appears in Leon-Dufour's book, *Resurrection and the Message of Easter*. In this volume he makes the distinction between "official appearances," which are more public and important, and "private appearances" to the women, that are of much less importance. This argument appears on page 71 of his book.

5. Francis Schüssler Fiorenza, *Foundational Theology: Jesus and the Church* (New York: Crossroad, 1984), 29.

6. Buttrick, *The Mystery and the Passion*, 16–17.

7. Kenan B. Osborne, *The Resurrection of Jesus: New Considerations for Its Theological Interpretation* (New York/Mahwah, N.J.: Paulist Press, 1997), 15. Used by permission. Osborne uses Bertold Klappert's categories from his 1967 book *Diskussion um Kreuz und Auferstehung* and restates them in terms of questions. He then explores these questions on pages 15–25.

8. See Leon-Dufour, *Resurrection and the Message of Easter*, 251; Pheme Perkins, *Resurrection: New Testament Witness* (Garden City, N.Y.: Doubleday & Company, Inc., 1984), 84–95; Thorwald Lorenzen, *Resurrection and Discipleship: Interpretive Models, Biblical Reflections, Theological Consequences* (Maryknoll, N.Y.: Orbis Books, 1995), 167–80; and Marianne Sawicki, *Seeing the Lord: Resurrection and Early Christian Practices* (Minneapolis: Fortress Press, 1994), 77–94.

9. Osborne, *The Resurrection of Jesus*, 38.

10. Sawicki, *Seeing the Lord*, 93.

11. Song, *Jesus, the Crucified People*, 13.

12. Leon-Dufour, *Resurrection and the Message of Easter*, 17.

13. Lorenzen, *Resurrection and Discipleship*, 146.

14. Osborne, *The Resurrection of Jesus*, 73.

15. Casaldáliga and Vigil, *Political Holiness*, 80.

16. Song, *Jesus and the Reign of God* (Minneapolis: Fortress Press, 1993), 287.

17. Juan Luis Segundo, *The Historical Jesus of the Synoptics* (Maryknoll, N.Y.: Orbis Books, 1985), 119–49.

18. Ibid., 90.

19. Ibid., 119–33.

20. Ibid., 134–49.

21. Ibid., 136.

22. Ibid., 141.

23. Fiorenza, *Foundational Theology*, 37.

24. Robert H. Smith, *Easter Gospels*, 29.

25. Osborne, *The Resurrection of Jesus*, 51–52.

26. Buttrick, *The Mystery and the Passion*, 46.

27. Sobrino, *Archbishop Romero: Memories and Reflections* (Maryknoll, N.Y.: Orbis Books, 1990), 208.

28. Fiorenza, *Foundational Theology*, 38.

29. Jack Pantaleo, "The Opened Tomb," *The Other Side*, vol. 28, no. 2 (March–April 1992): 8.

30. Joyce Hollyday, *Clothed with the Sun: Biblical Women, Social Justice and Us*, (Louisville: Westminster John Knox Press, 1994), 224–25.

Chapter 5: Untying Grave Clothes

1. Janet Morley, ed., *Bread of Tomorrow: Prayers for the Church Year* (Maryknoll, N.Y.: Orbis Books, 1992), 102–03.

2. This is quoted from the spoken liturgy at Spirit of the Lakes United Church of Christ in Minneapolis, Minn. We follow this liturgy every Sunday.

3. Marilyn Bennett Alexander and James Preston, *We Were Baptized Too: Claiming God's Grace for Lesbians and Gays* (Louisville: Westminster John Knox Press, 1996), 23.

4. Boff, *When Theology Listens to the Poor*, 132.

5. Sharon D. Welch, *A Feminist Ethic of Risk* (Minneapolis: Fortress Press, 1990), 75.

6. Heyward, *Touching Our Strength*, 33.

7. A description of Paul T. Granlund's "Resurrection," as it appears in *Imaging the Word*, 185.

8. Brock, *Journeys by Heart*; Heyward, *Speaking Of Christ*; Kyung, *Struggle to Be the Sun Again*; Isasi-Díaz, *Mujerista Theology: A Theology for the Twenty-first Century* (Maryknoll, N.Y.: Orbis Press, 1996).

9. This experience happened in the context of a national meeting of The Association of Practical Theology held in Los Angeles in 1993.

10. Melanie A. May, *A Body Knows: A Theopoetics of Death and Resurrection* (New York: Continuum, 1995), 39.

11. This happened on May 30, 1993, in a Roman Catholic parish in Managua, Nicaragua. These words are from a song in the Nicaraguan Peasant Mass. Flavio Galo has since been murdered.

12. These words were spoken by Norma Galo in the context of that same liturgy.

13. Heyward, *Touching Our Strength*, 47.

14. May, *A Body Knows*, 67–68.

15. Ibid., 68.

16. Ibid.

17. Nancy L. Eiesland, *The Disabled God: Toward a Liberatory Theology of Disability* (Nashville: Abingdon Press, 1994), 13.

18. Ibid., 70.

19. Ibid., 66.

20. Ibid., 39.

21. Ibid., 107.

22. Kathy Black, *A Healing Homiletic: Preaching and Disability* (Nashville: Abingdon Press, 1996), 42.

23. Mitsuye Yamada, *Desert Run: Poems and Stories* (Latham, N.Y.: Kitchen Table: Women of Color Press, 1988). This information about the author is found at the back of her book.

24. Yamada, *Camp Notes and Other Writings* (New Brunswick, N.J.: Rutgers University Press, 1992), 53–54. Used by permission.

25. William Minoru Hohri, *Repairing America: An Account of the Movement for Japanese-American Redress* (Pullman: Washington State University Press, 1988).

26. Jane Adams Spahr, Kathryn Poethig, Selisse Berry, Melinda V. McLain, ed., *Called Out: The Voices and Gifts of Lesbian, Gay, Bisexual, and Transgendered Presby terians* (Gaithersburg, Md.: ChiRho Press, 1995), 242 –43.

27. James Melvin Washington, *A Testament of Hope: The Essential Writings of Martin Luther King, Jr.* (San Francisco: Harper & Row, 1986), 292–93. Used by permission.

28. Brown and Parker, "And God So Loved the World," 28.

29. Boff, *Passion of Christ, Passion of the World* (Maryknoll, N.Y.: Orbis Press, 1987), 3.

30. Dorothee Söelle, *Strength of the Weak: Toward a Christian Feminist Identity* (Philadelphia: The Westminster Press, 1984), 76.

31. Martin Duberman, *Stonewall* (New York: A Plume Book, 1993), xvii.

32. JoAnn Gibson Robinson, *The Montgomery Bus Boycott and the Women Who Started It* (Knoxville: The University of Tennessee Press, 1987), 3.

33. Gary Remafedi, *Death by Denial: Studies of Suicide in Gay and Lesbian Teenagers* (Boston: Alyson Publications, 1994), 15.

34. Mark Carlson, Marion Bauer, Lori Lippert, Jeff Turner, *Coming Out, Coming Home*, a play written and produced in 1991 by members of Spirit of the Lakes United Church of Christ, Minneapolis, Minnesota, 47–48. Used by permission.

35. Chris Glaser, *Come Home: Reclaiming Spirituality and Community as Gay Men and Lesbians* (San Francisco: Harper & Row, 1990), 11.

36. Nancy Wilson, *Our Tribe: Queer Folks, God, Jesus, and the Bible* (San Francisco: HarperSanFrancisco, 1995), 43.

37. Julia Penelope and Susan J. Wolfe, ed., *The Original Coming Out Stories* (Freedom, Calif.: The Crossing Press, 1980), 3–4.

38. Melanie Morrison, *The Grace of Coming Home: Spirituality, Sexuality, and the Struggle for Justice* (Cleveland: The Pilgrim Press, 1995), 39.

39. Heyward, *Touching Our Strength*, 36.

40. Quoted from a student in one of my classes. Much to my embarrassment, I do not remember the specific student's name.

41. Sweet Honey In The Rock, "Patchwork Quilt" from *In This Land* (Redway, Calif.: Earthbeat Records, 1992). Used by permission.

42. Sharon D. Welch, *Communities of Resistance and Solidarity: A Feminist Theology of Liberation* (Maryknoll, N.Y.: Orbis Books, 1985), 36.

43. Ibid., 39.

44. Ibid., 37.

45. Ibid., 39.

46. Sobrino, *Archbishop Romero: Memories and Reflections* (Maryknoll, N.Y.: Orbis Books, 1990), 204–05.

47. James R. Brockman, *Romero: A Life* (Maryknoll, N.Y.: Orbis Books, 1989), 248.

48. Sal Lopes, *The Wall: Images and Offerings from the Vietnam Veterans Memorial* (New York: Collins Publishers, 1987). This photo appears on the back cover of the book.

49. May, *A Body Knows*, 19.

50. Matilde Mellibrovsky, *Circle Over Death: Testimonies of the Mothers of the Plaza de Mayo* (Willimantic, Conn.: Curbstone Press, 1997).

51. Ibid., 82–83.

52. Ibid., 200–01.

53. Holly Near, "Ain't No Where You Can Run," from the album *Fire in the Rain* (Ukiah, Calif.: Redwood Records, 1981). Used by permission.

54. Brown and Parker, "For God So Loved the World," 28.

55. The scene is portrayed in the movie *Romero*, dir. John Dulgan, prod. United States Roman Catholic Church, 102 min. (Trimark Home Video, 1989). Used by permission.

56. Pantaleo, "The Opened Tomb," 8.